Birds & Butterflies
color by numbers

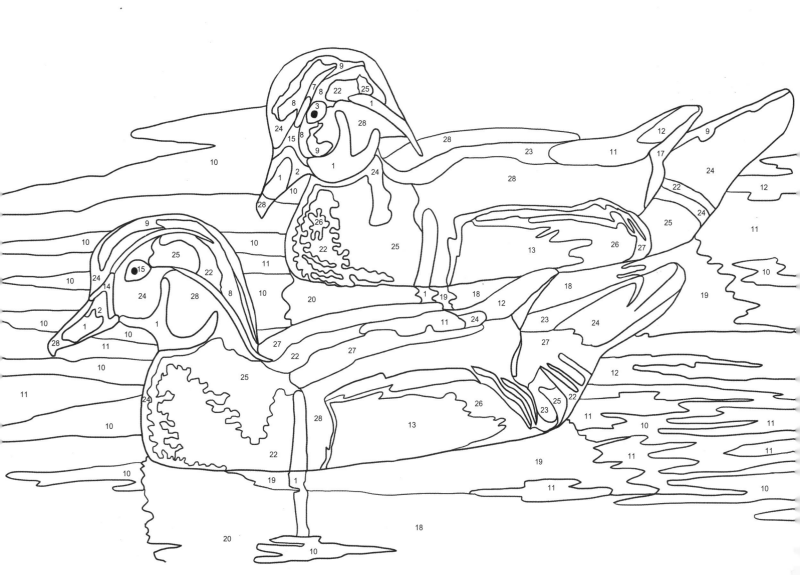

Birds & Butterflies
color by numbers

Arpad Olbey
and
Sara Storino

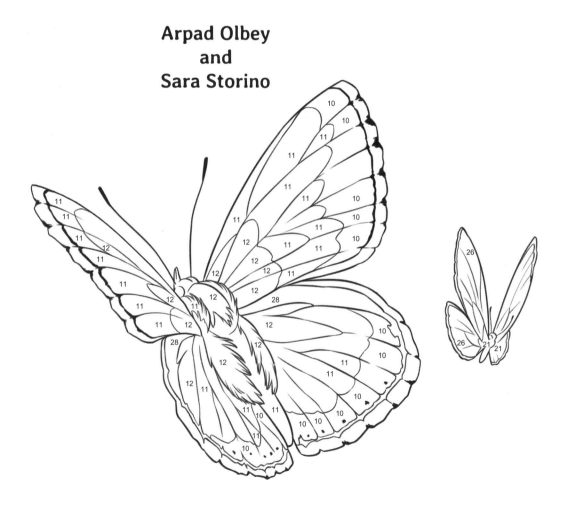

SIRIUS

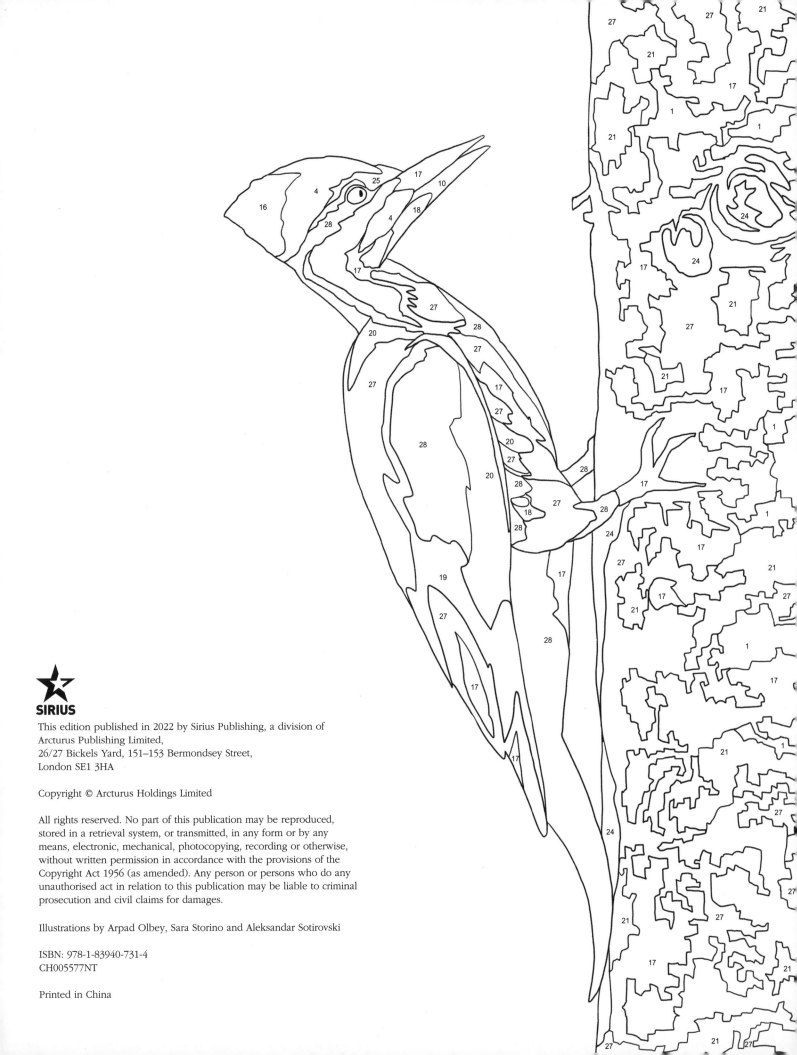

SIRIUS

This edition published in 2022 by Sirius Publishing, a division of
Arcturus Publishing Limited,
26/27 Bickels Yard, 151–153 Bermondsey Street,
London SE1 3HA

Illustrations by Arpad Olbey, Sara Storino and Aleksandar Sotirovski

ISBN: 978-1-83940-731-4
CH005577NT

Printed in China

INTRODUCTION

This book is dedicated to some of the most beautiful, colorful creatures on our planet: birds and butterflies. Blessed with the ability to fly, some birds can soar through the skies for days on end, while butterflies flit tirelessly from flower to flower during their short lives. In these pages you can color bird species from around the globe, from flamboyant flamingos and peacocks to Antarctic penguins and albatrosses. Butterfly species include the widespread peacock butterfly with its distinctive "eyes," and the rare and delicate Amazon angel with its translucent bluish wings. All birds and butterflies are shown in habitats where you might expect to find them, either in the wild, or in parks and gardens. If you wish to color something a little more whimsical, there are also several patterns based on birds and butterflies to be found at the end of the collection.

Each image is numbered so that, by matching your pencils as closely as possible to the numbered color key on the cover, you can build up an accurate depiction of the species shown. If there is no number, that means the area should be left white.

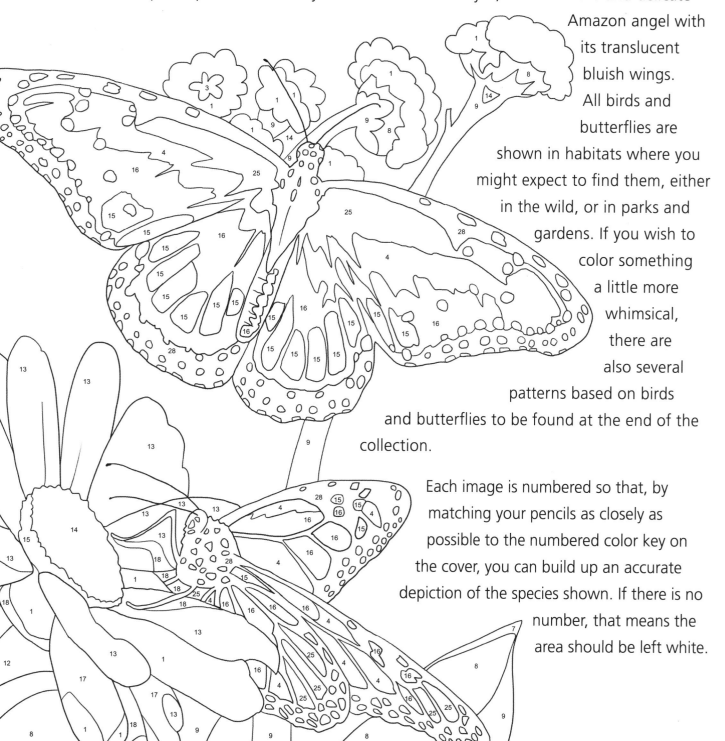

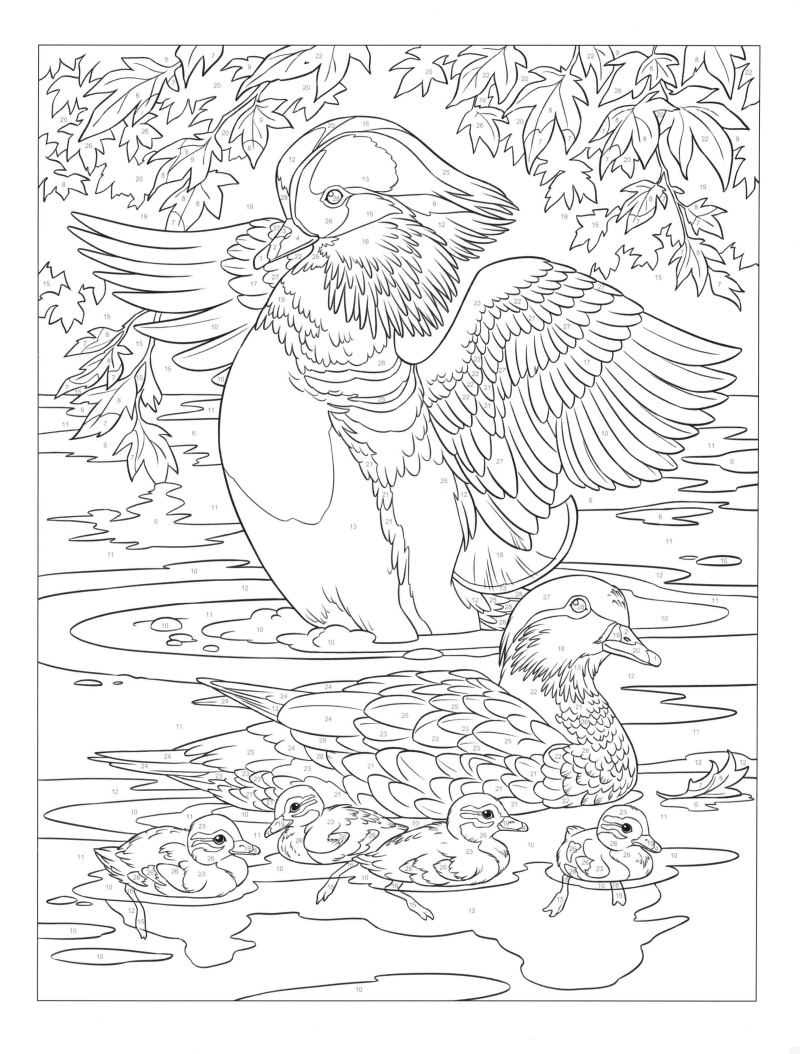

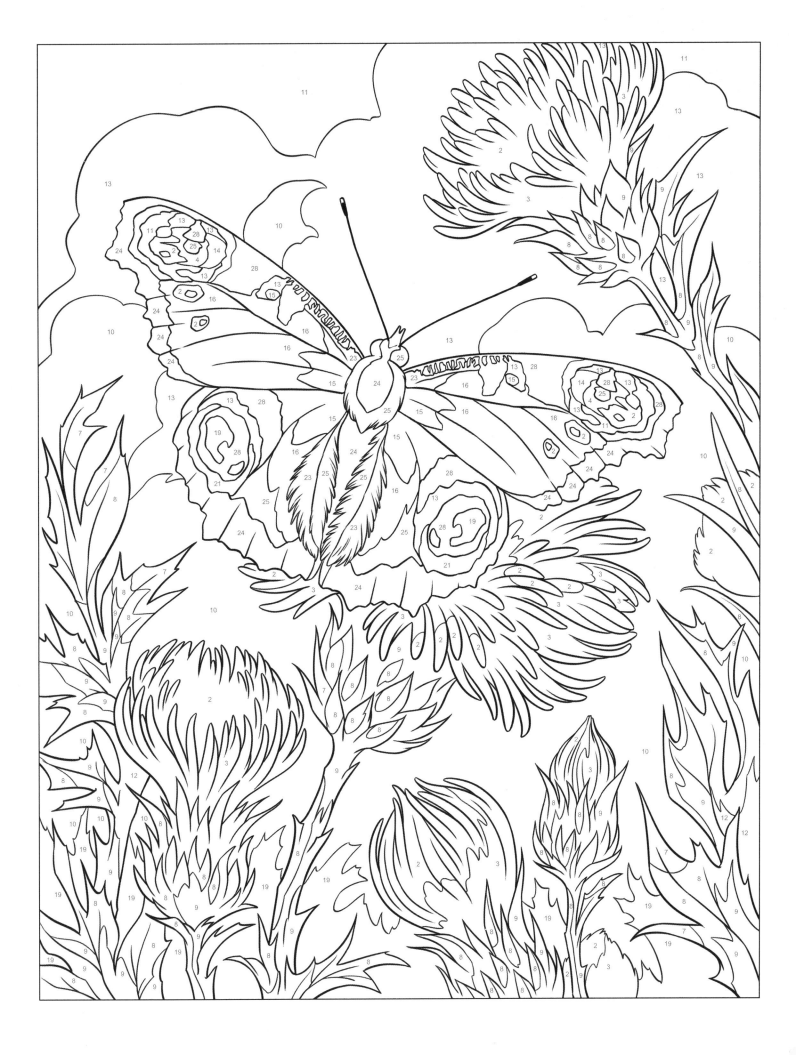

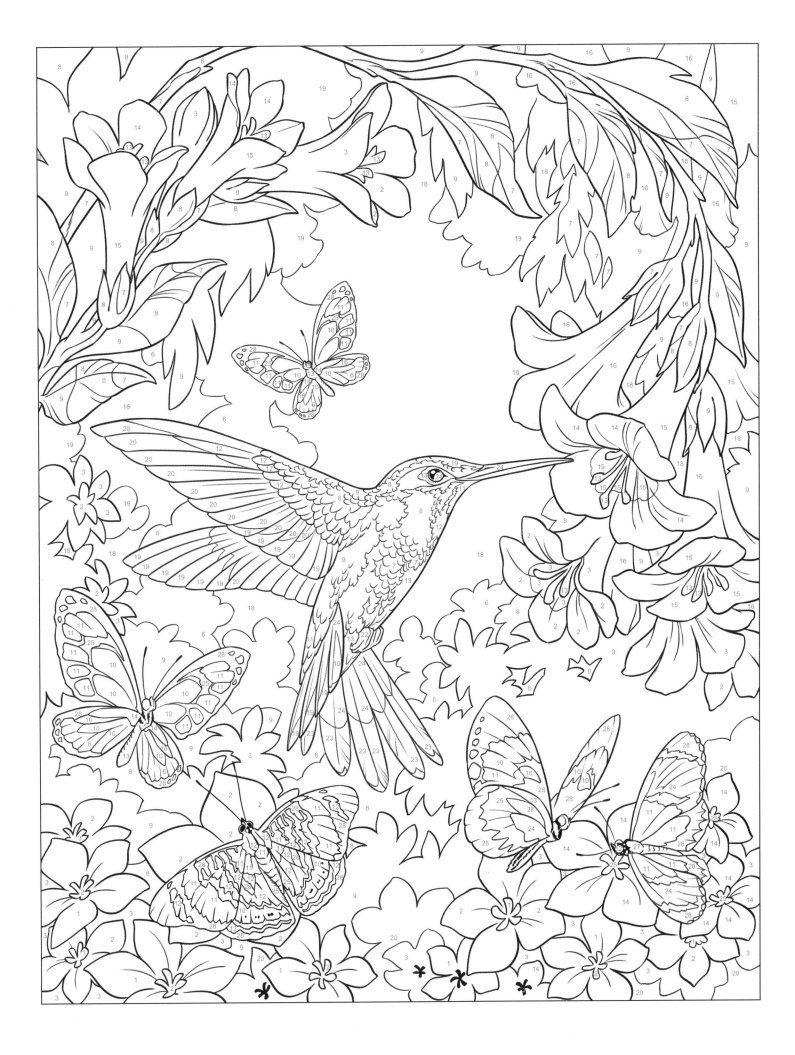

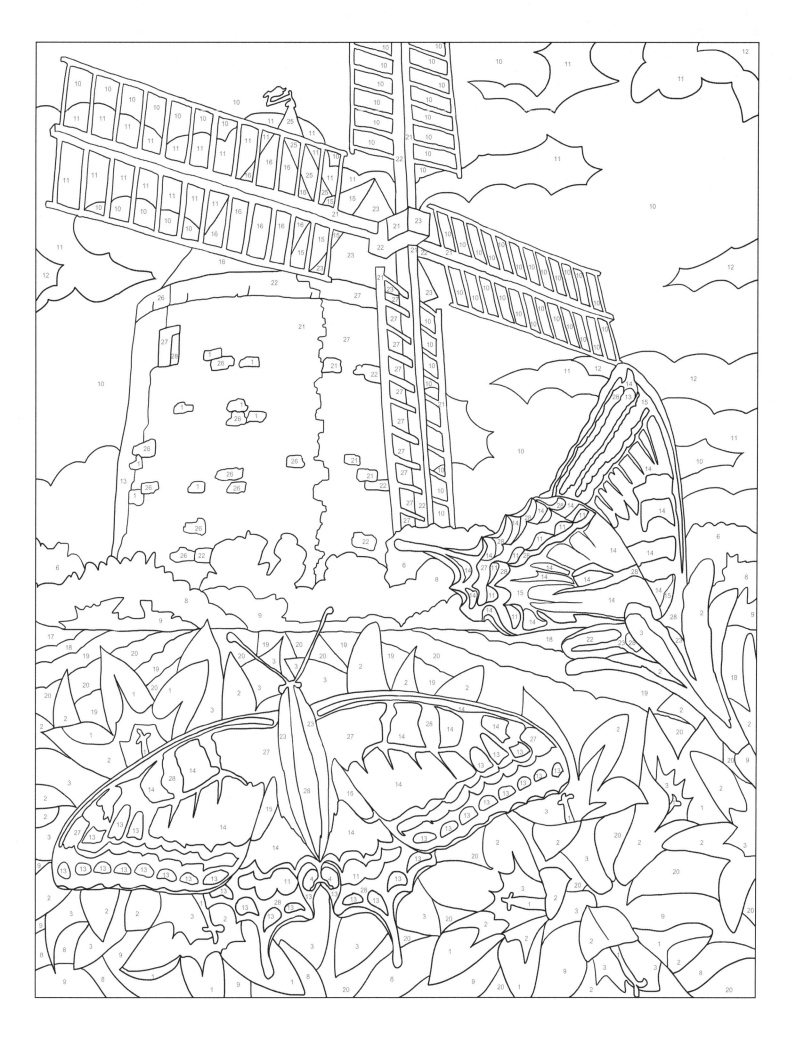

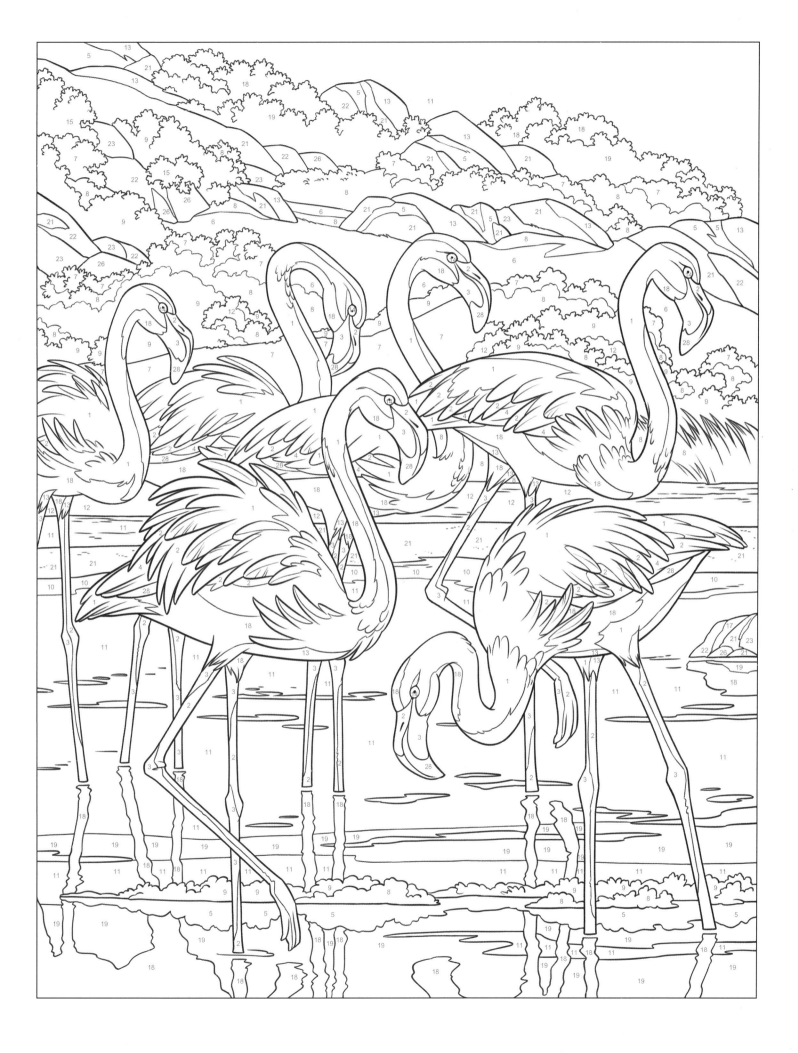

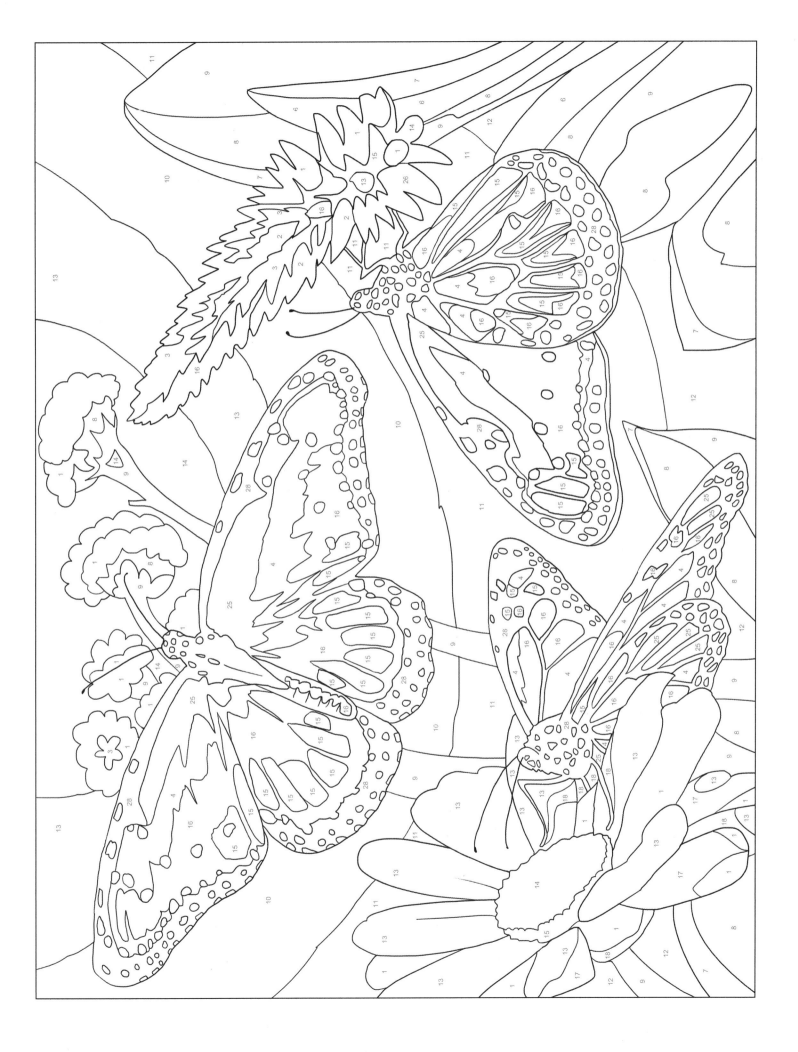

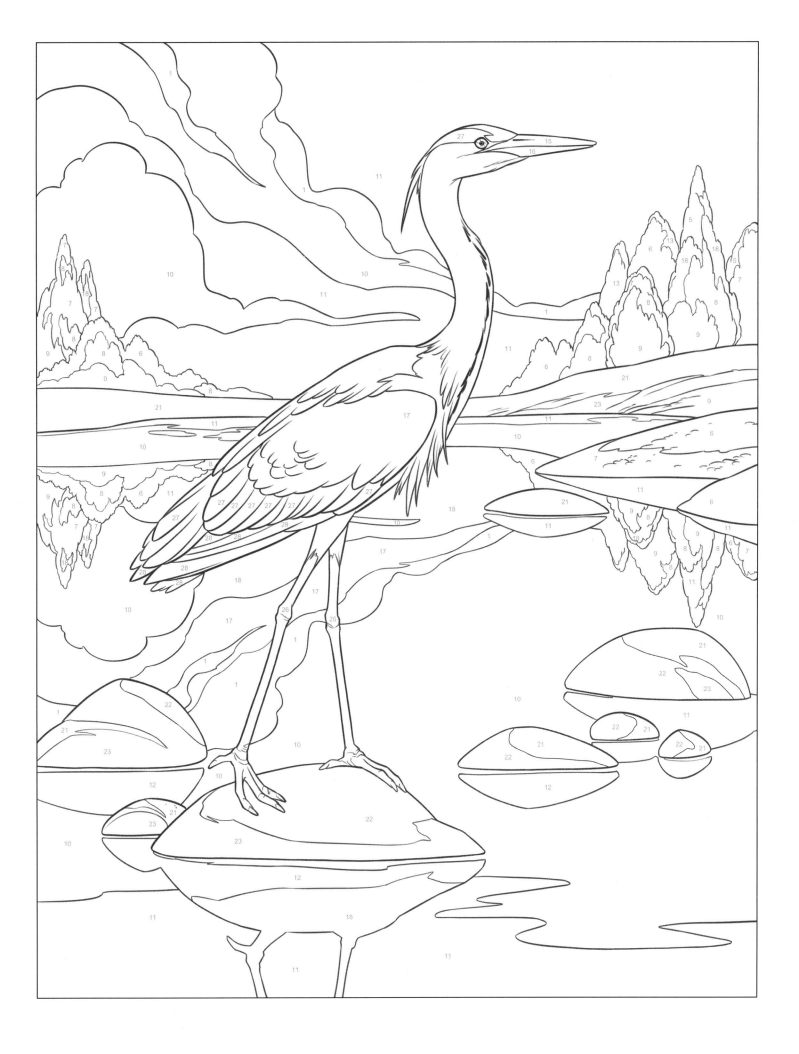

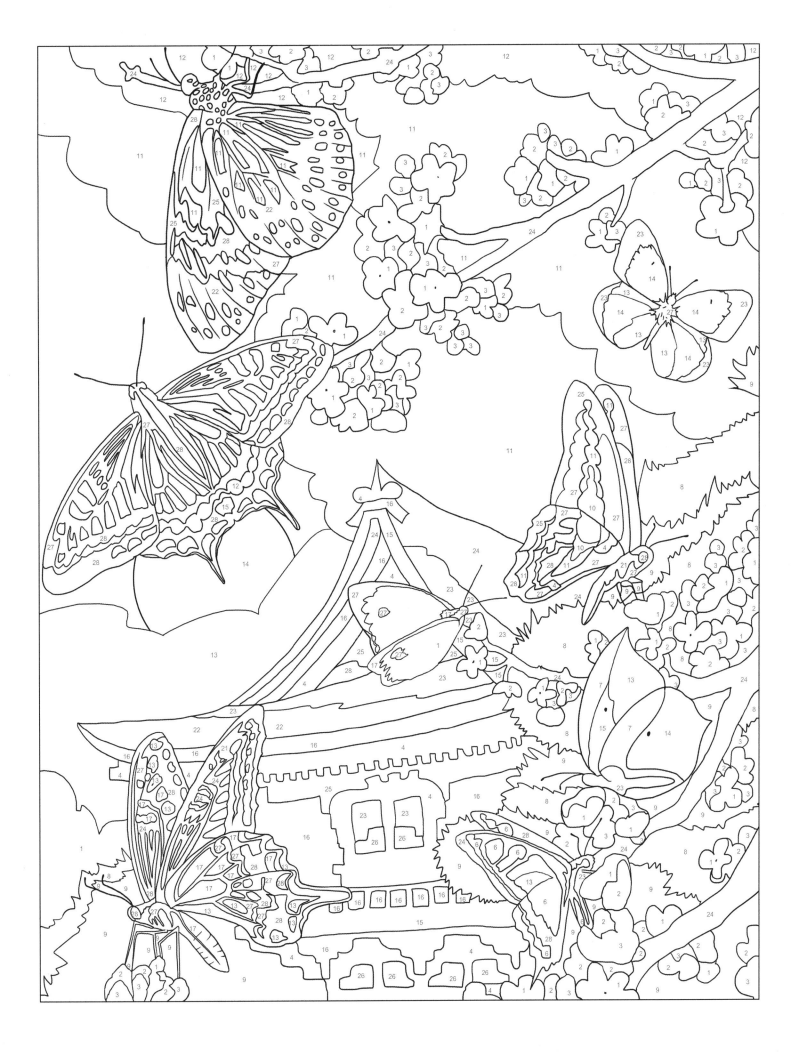

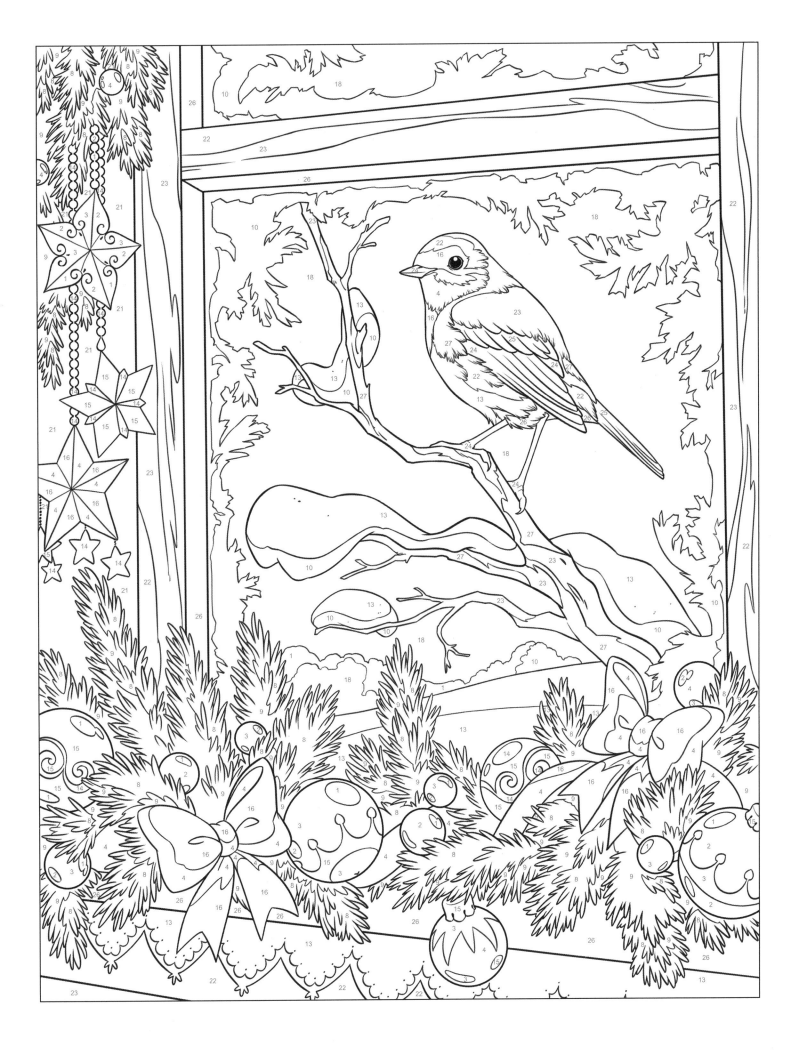

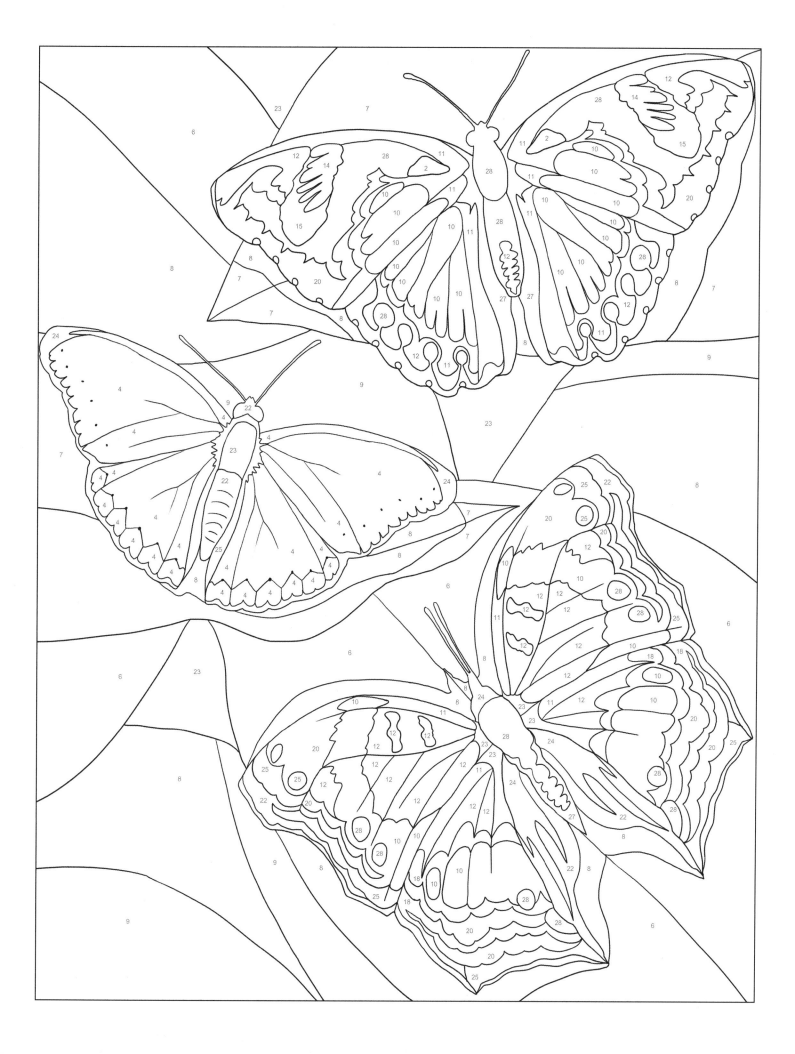

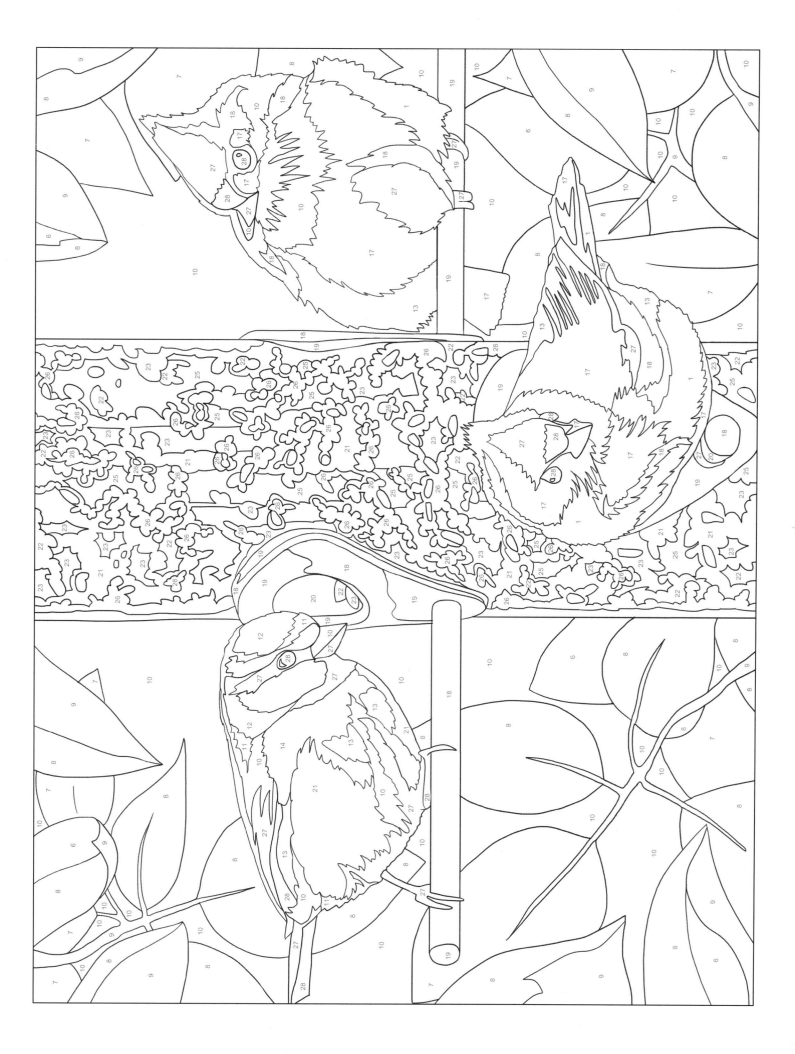

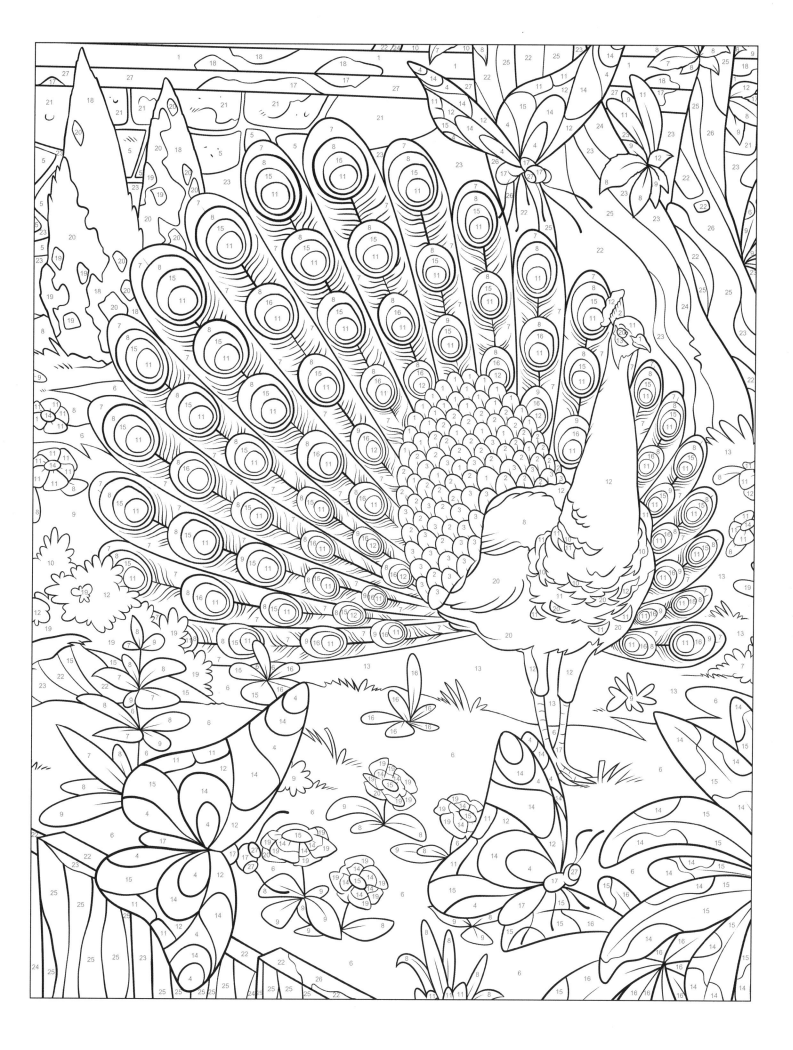

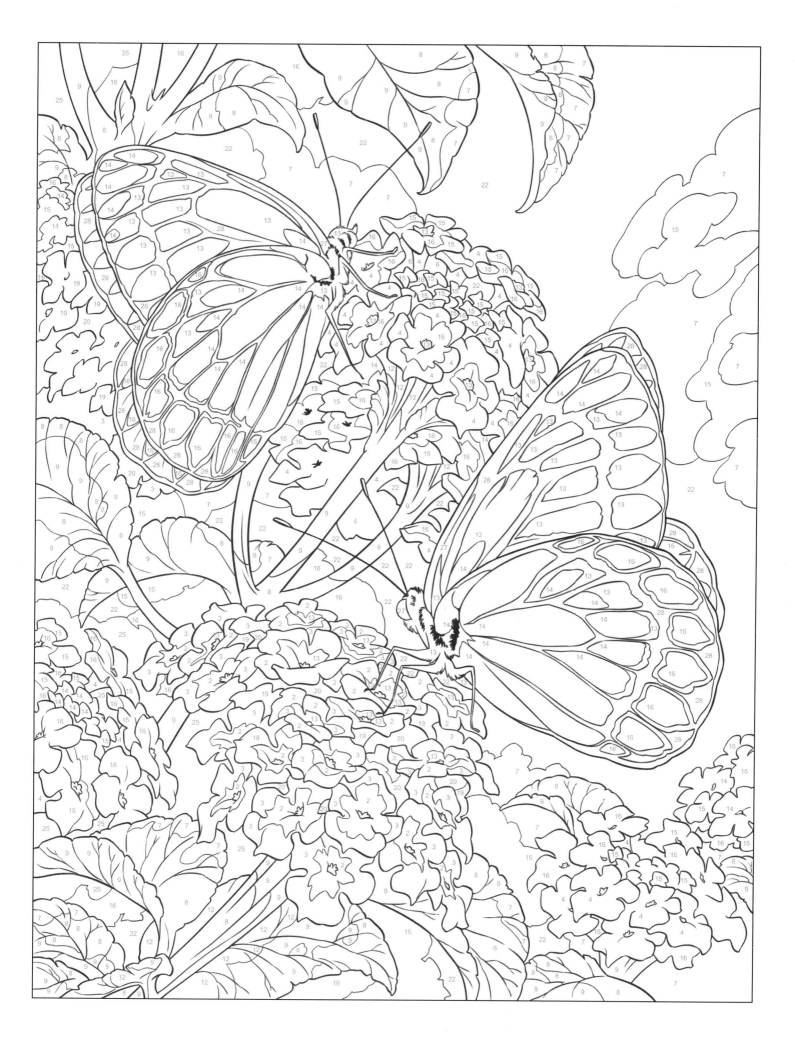

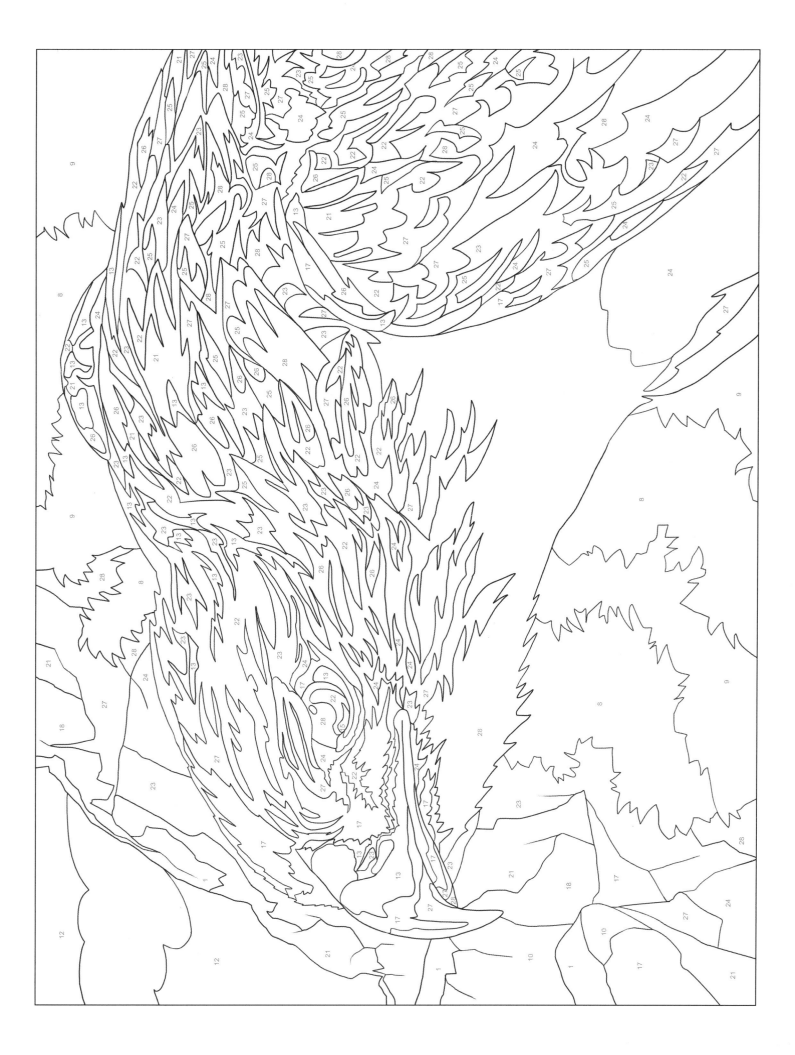

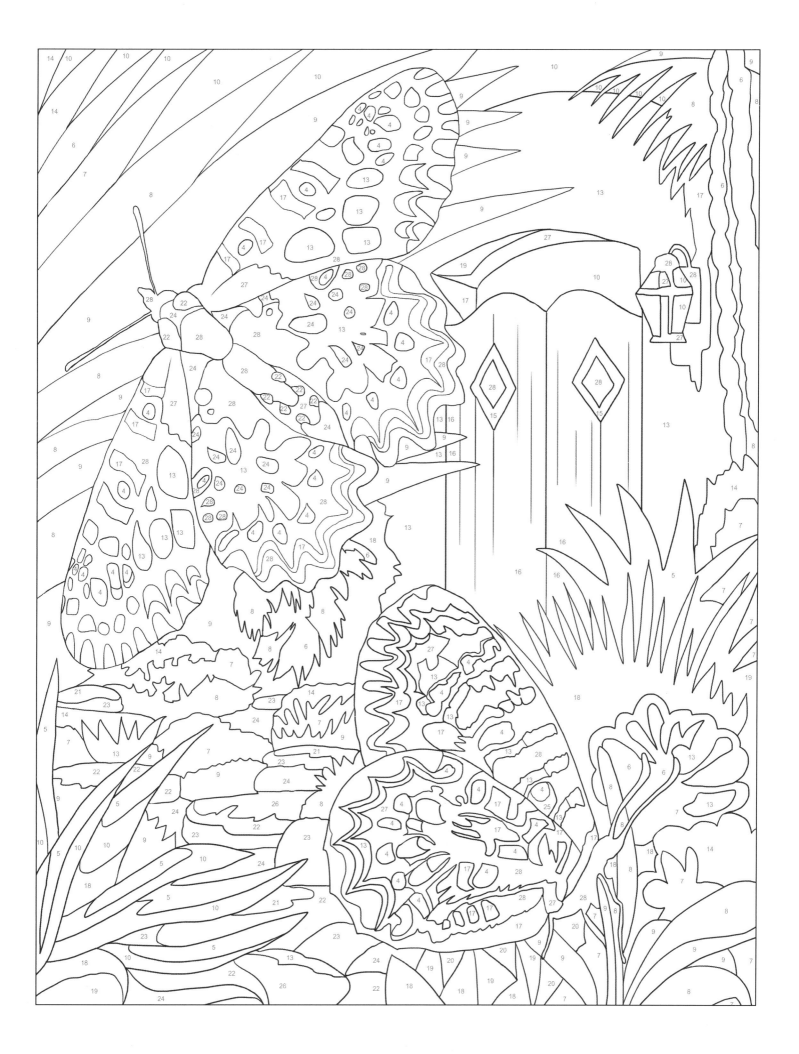

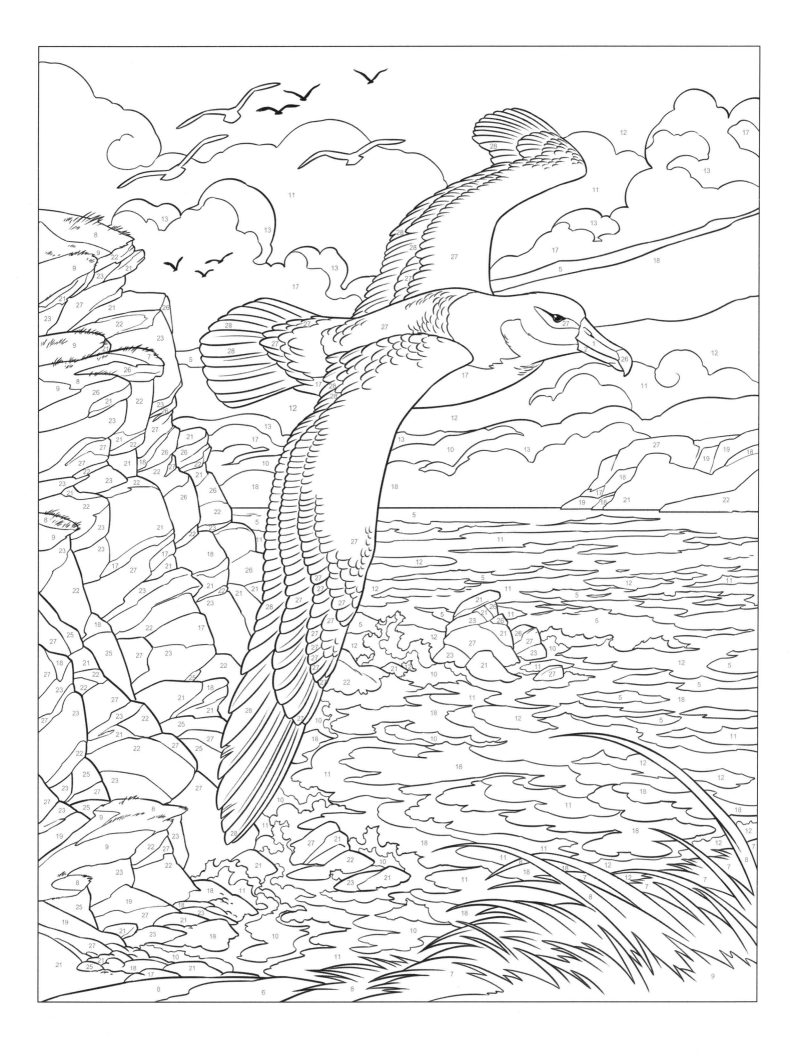

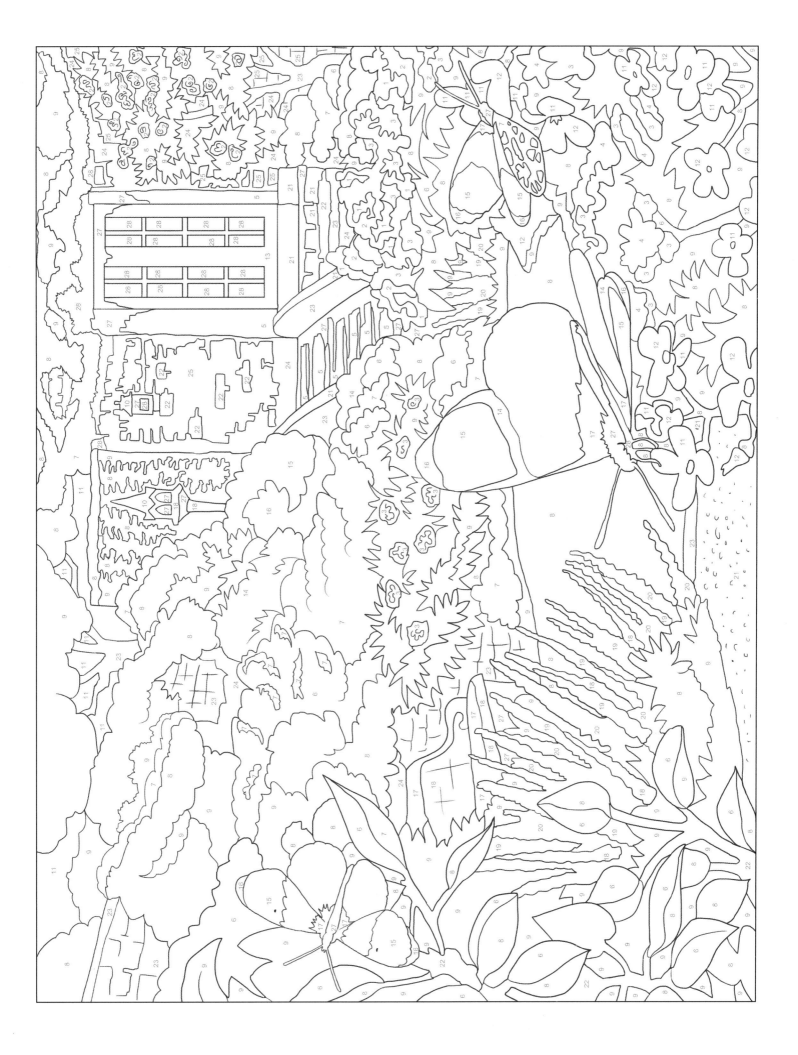

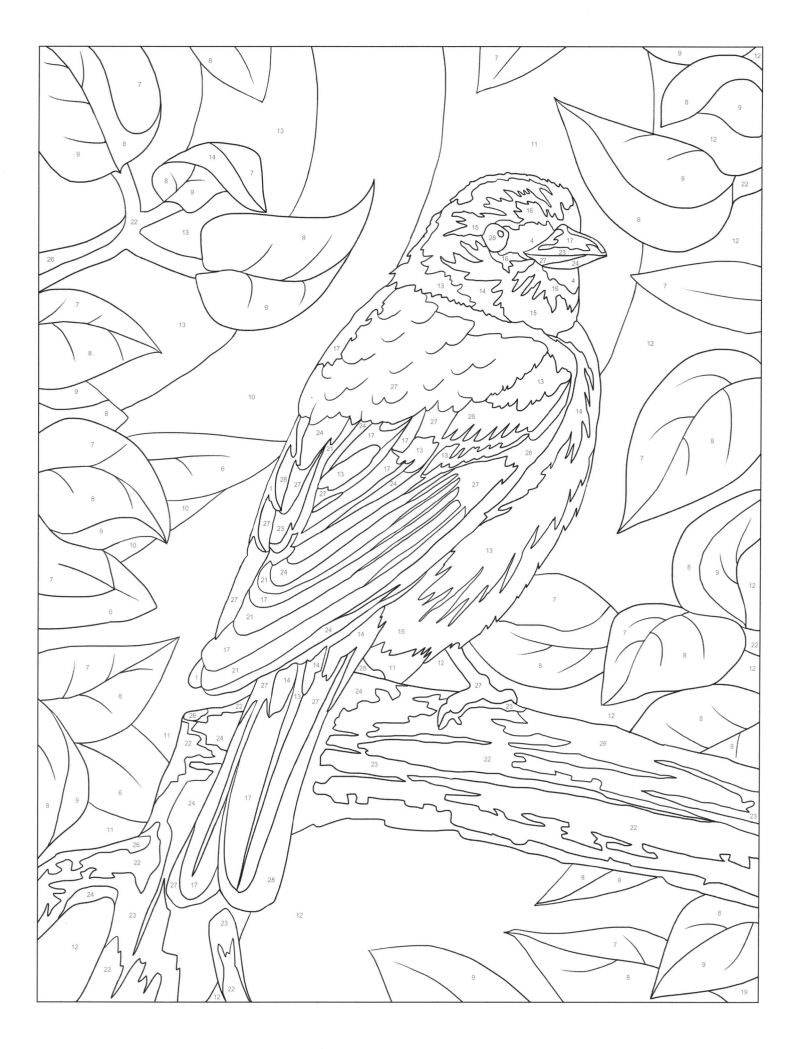

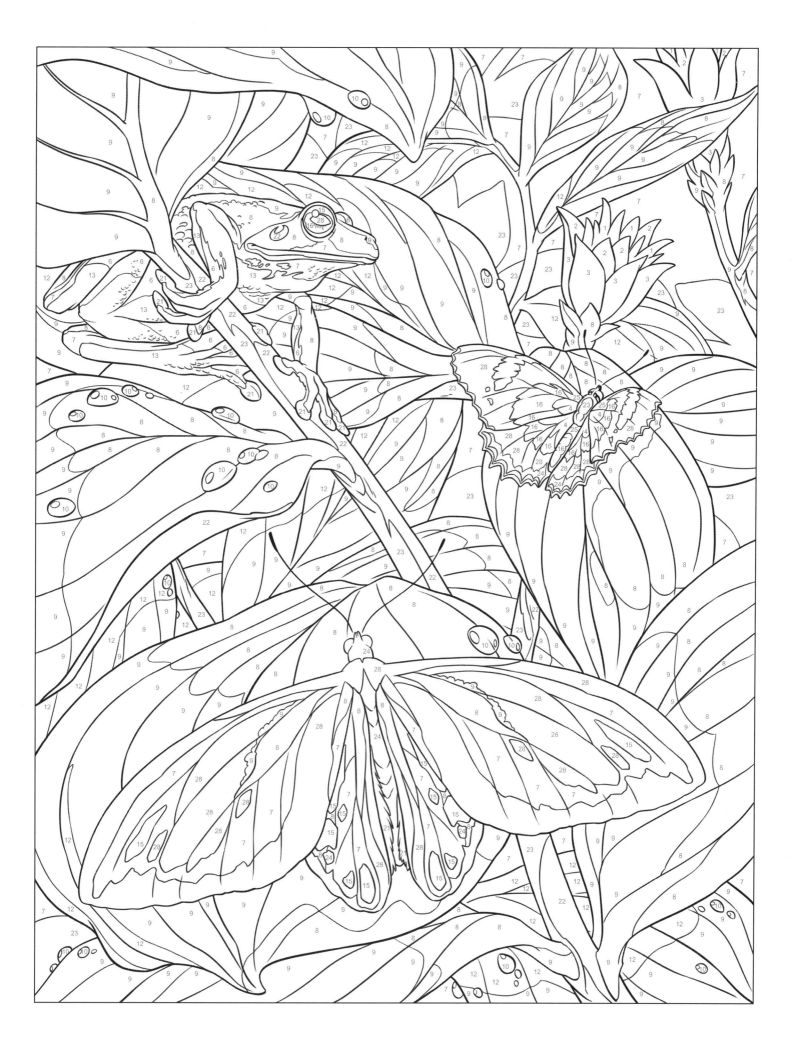

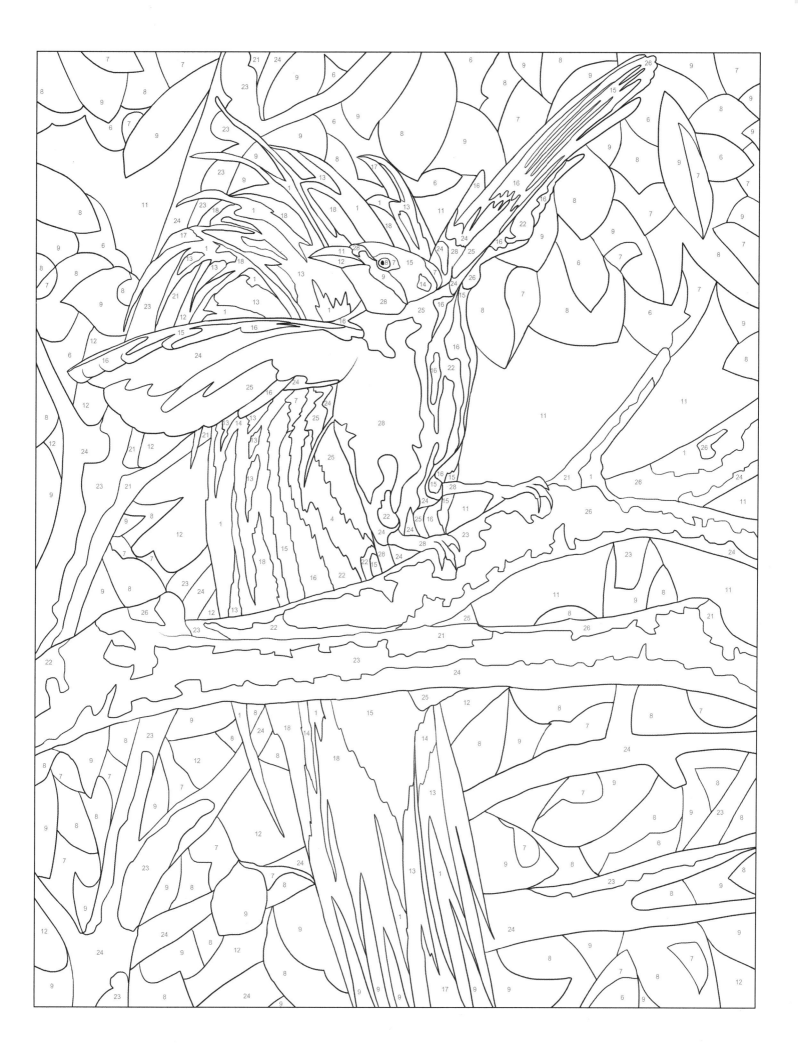

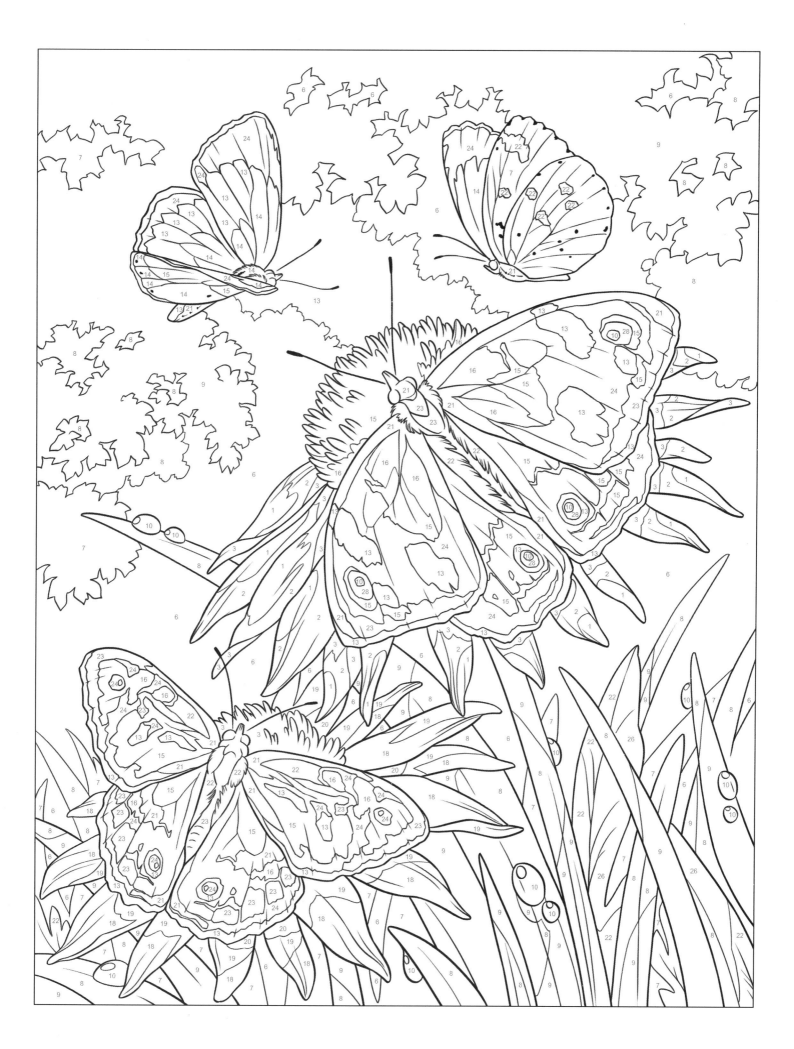

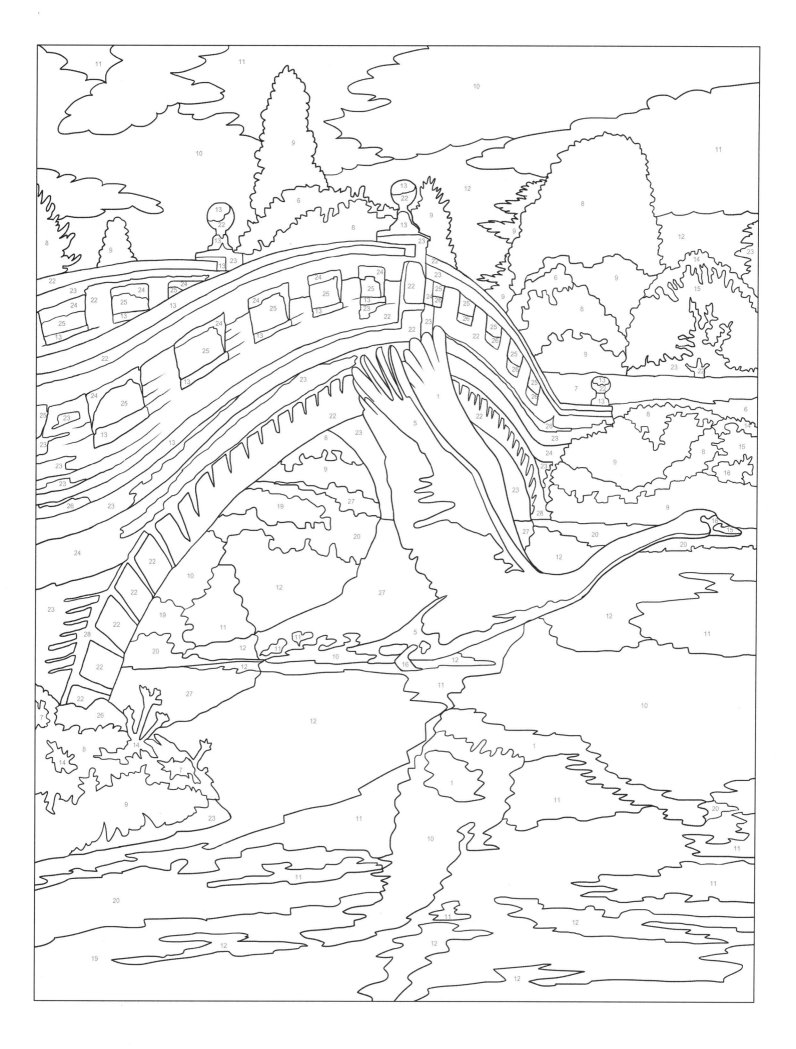

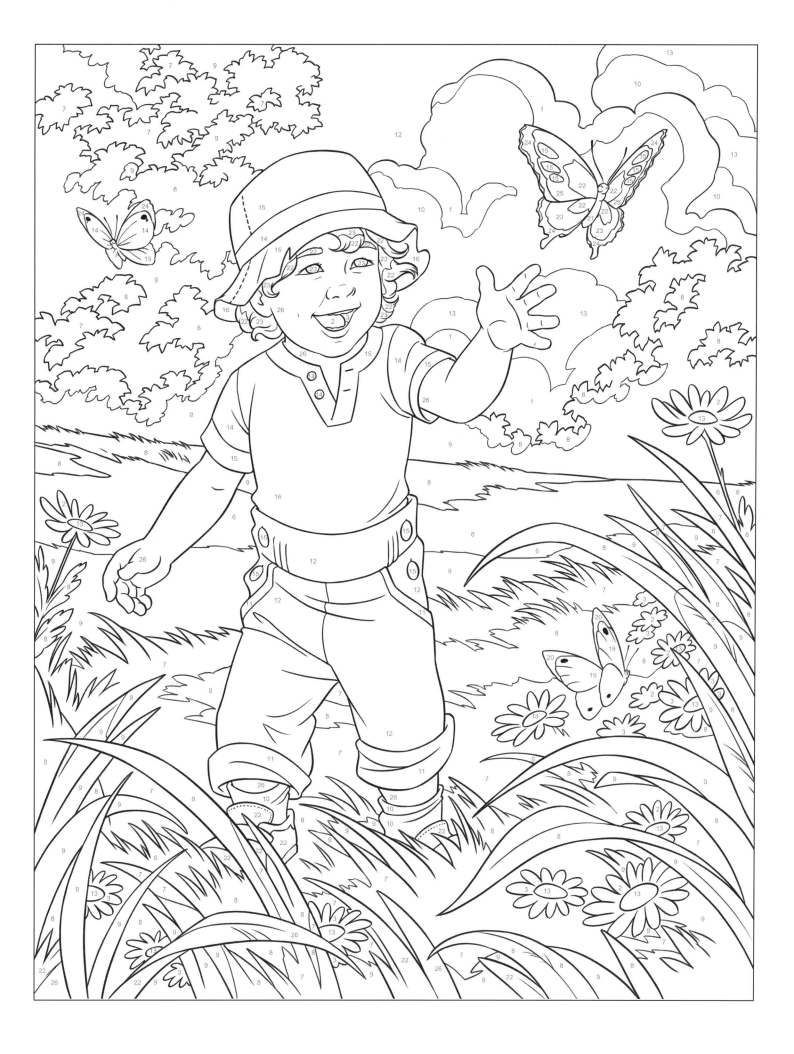

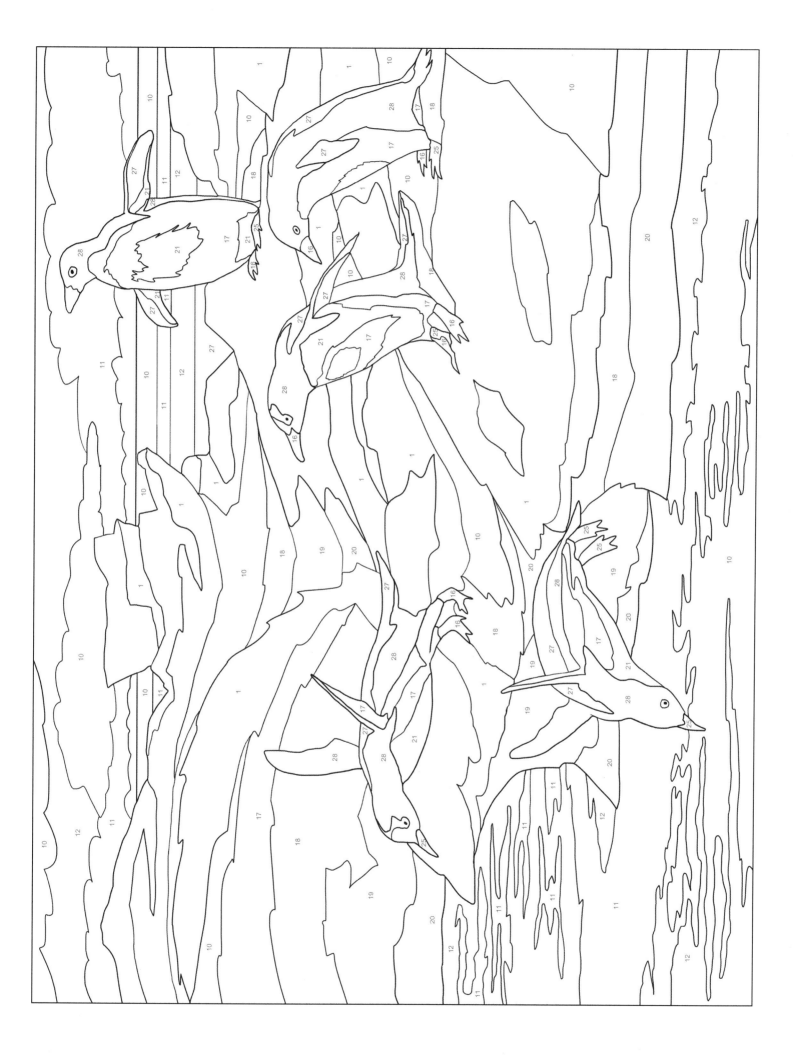

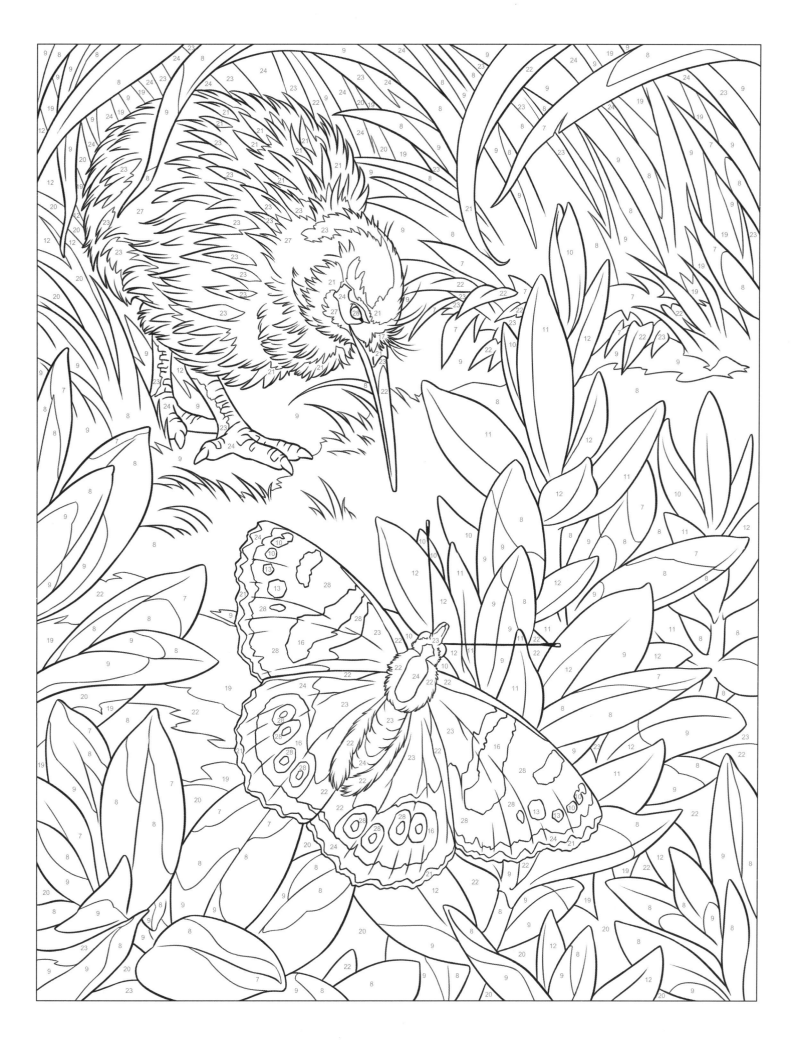

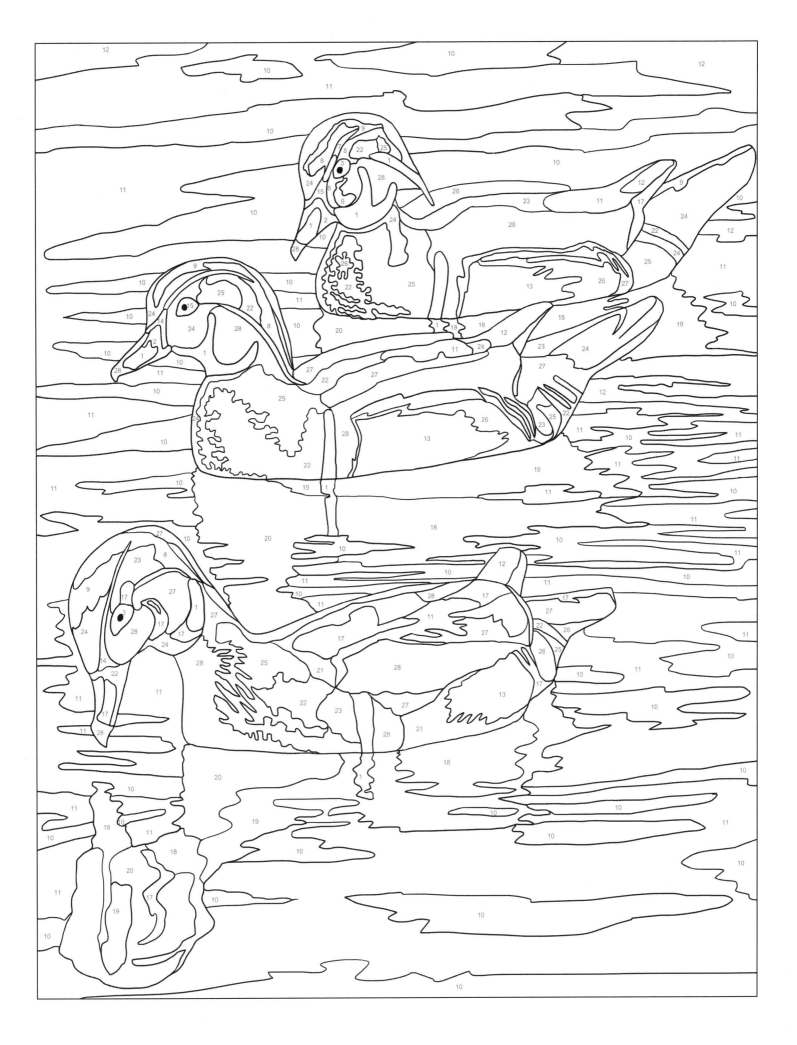

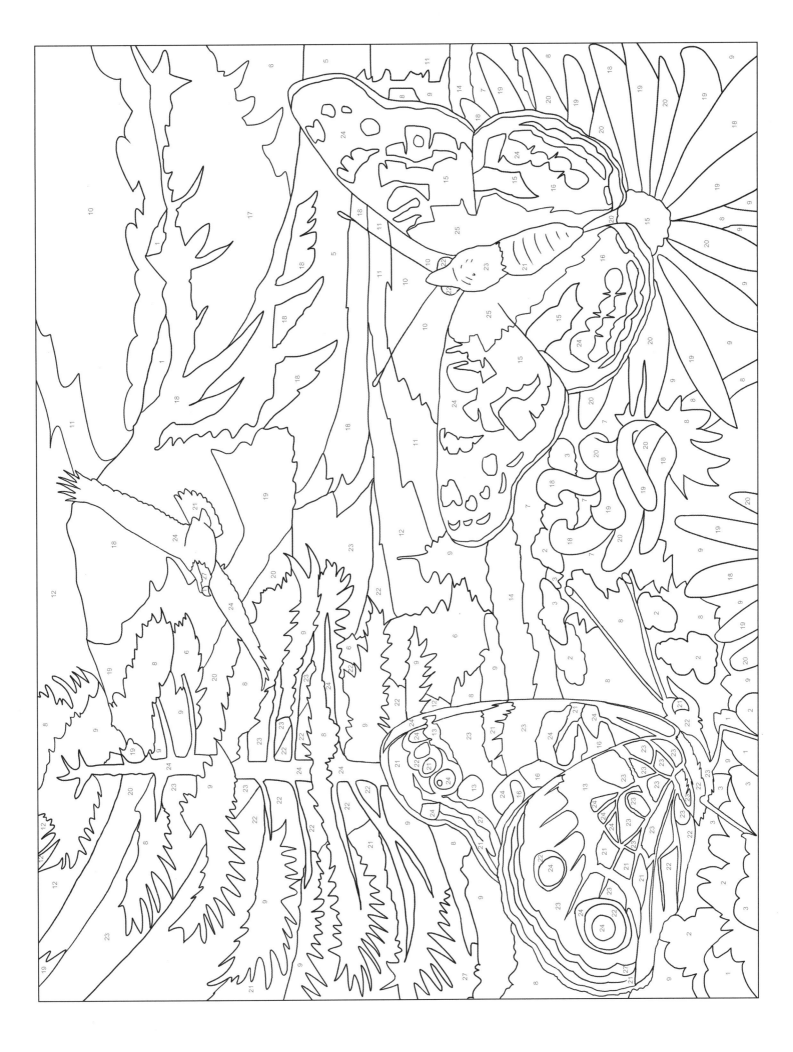

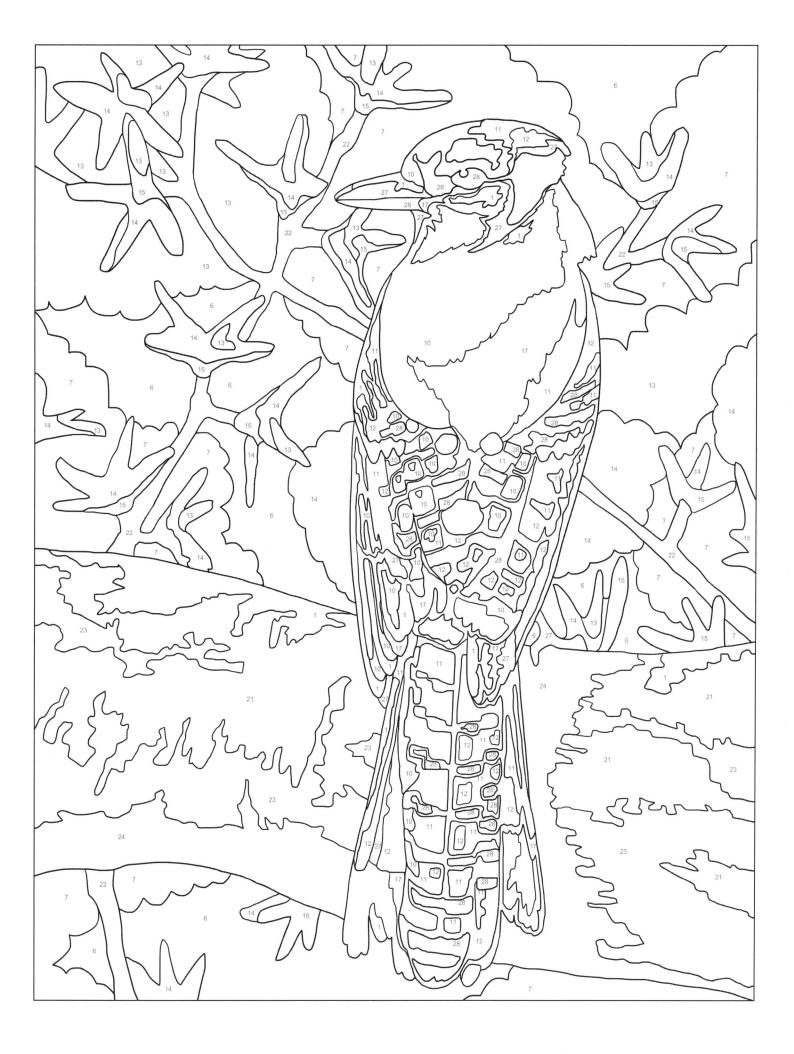

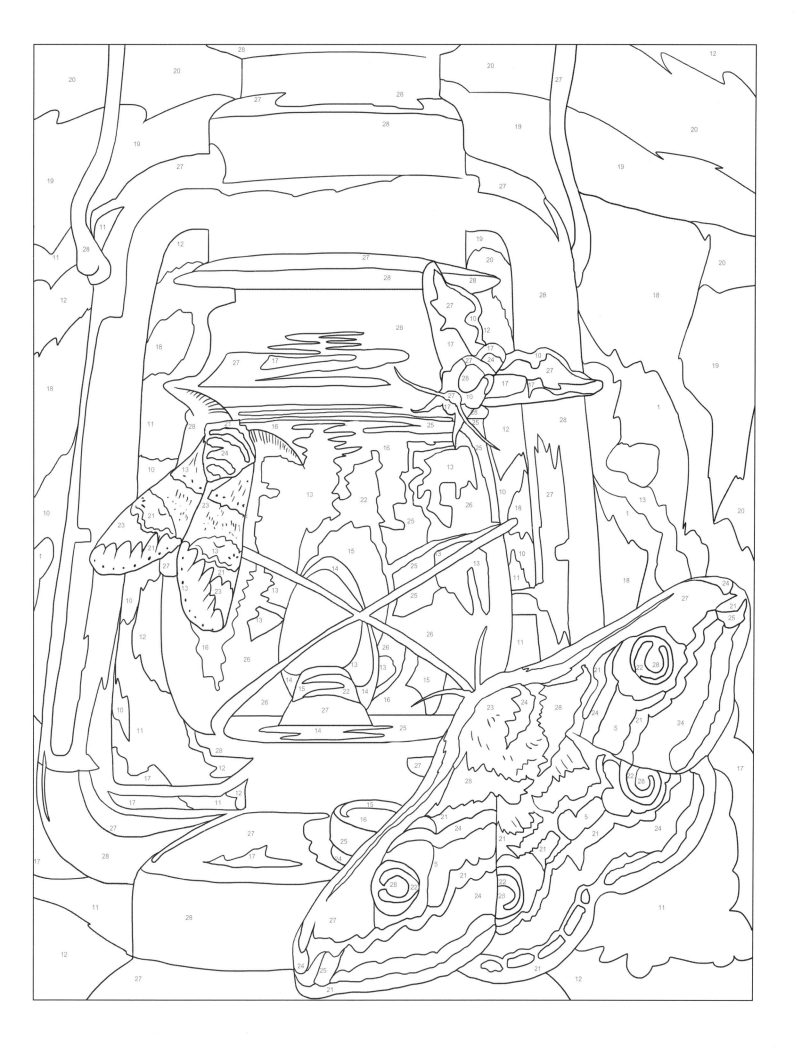

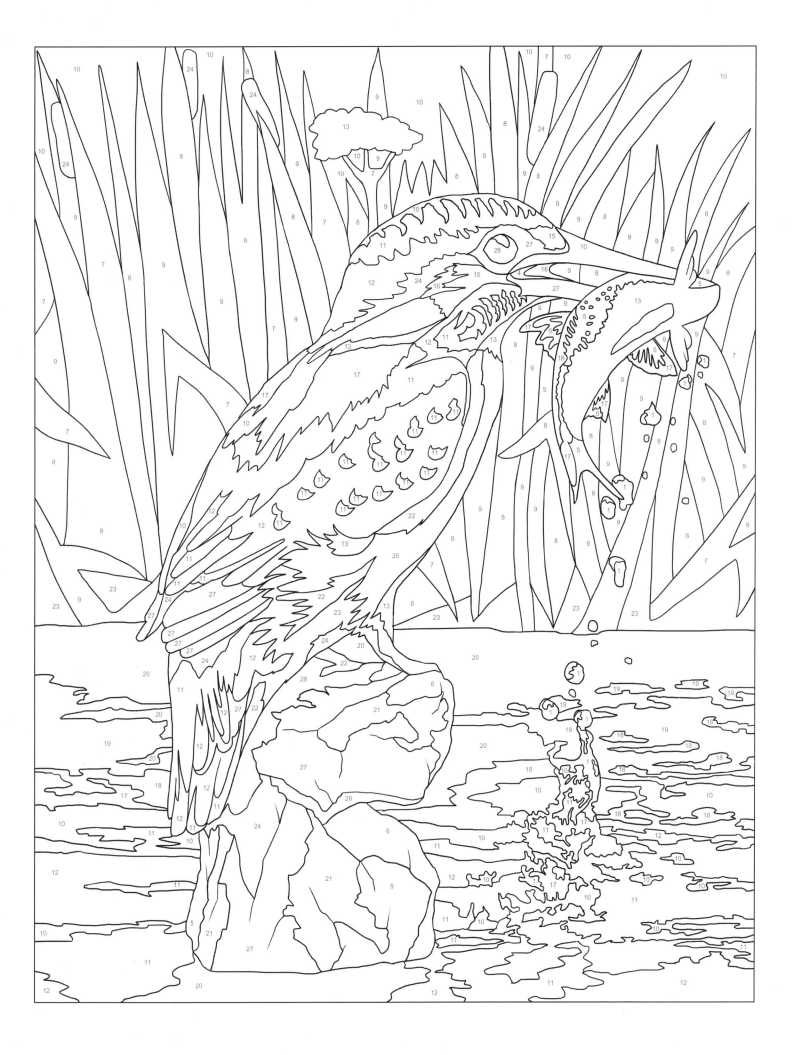

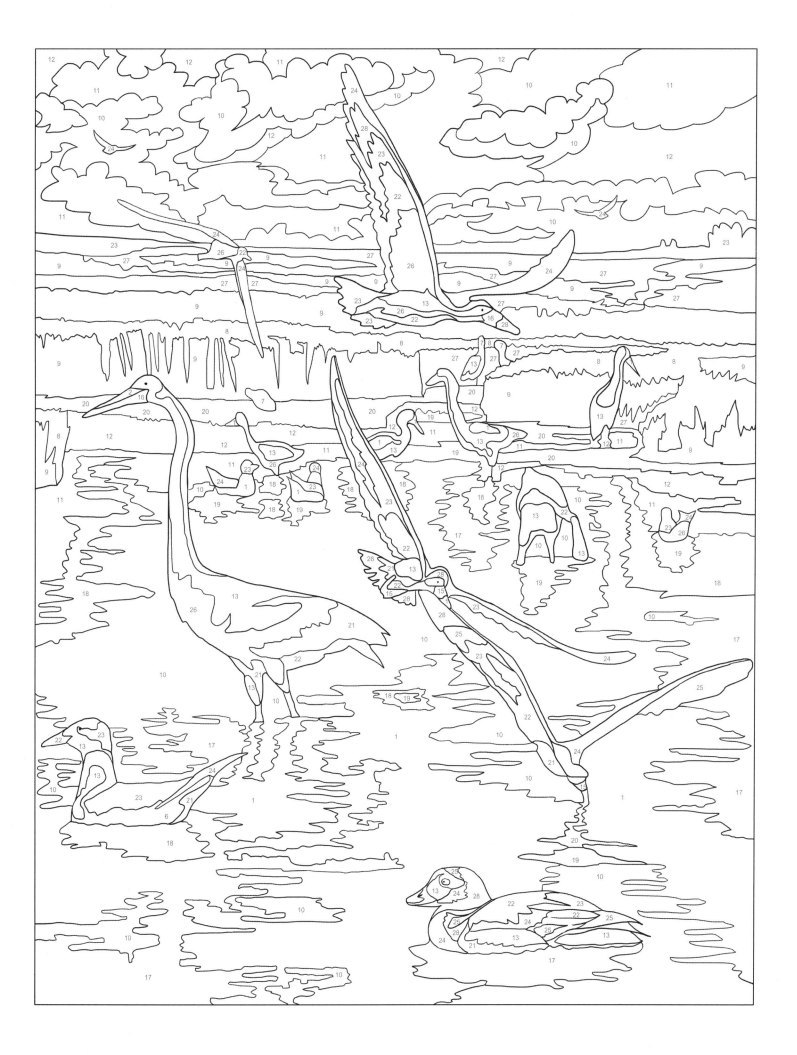

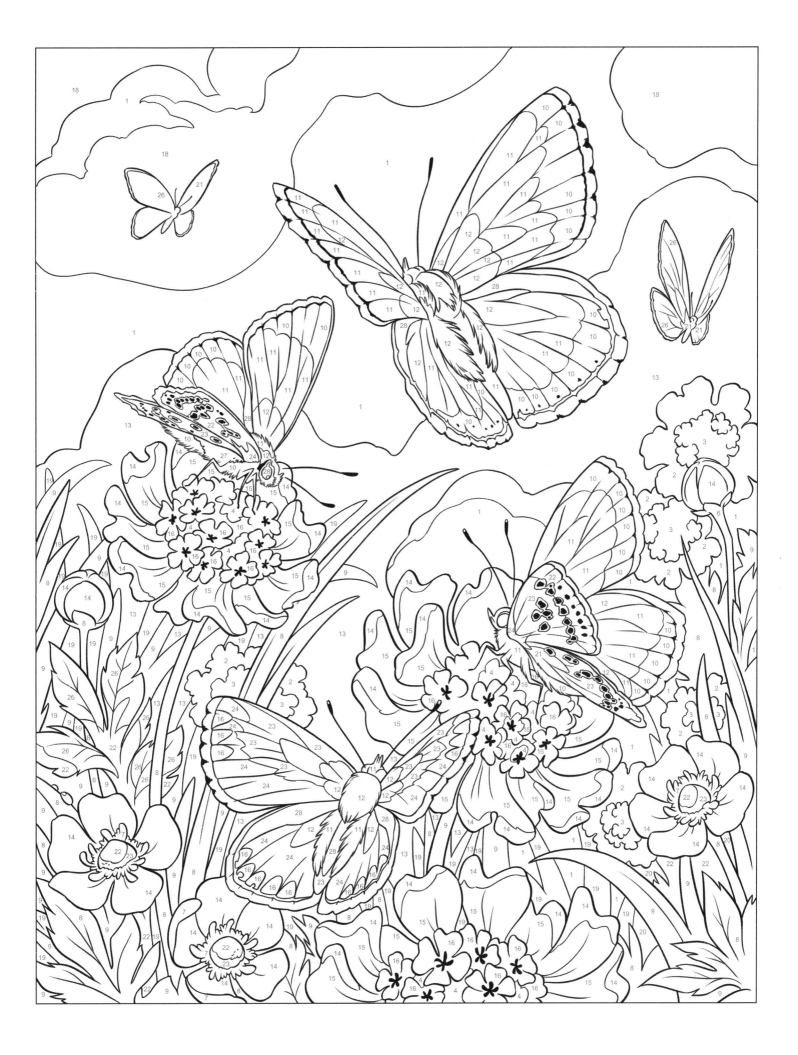

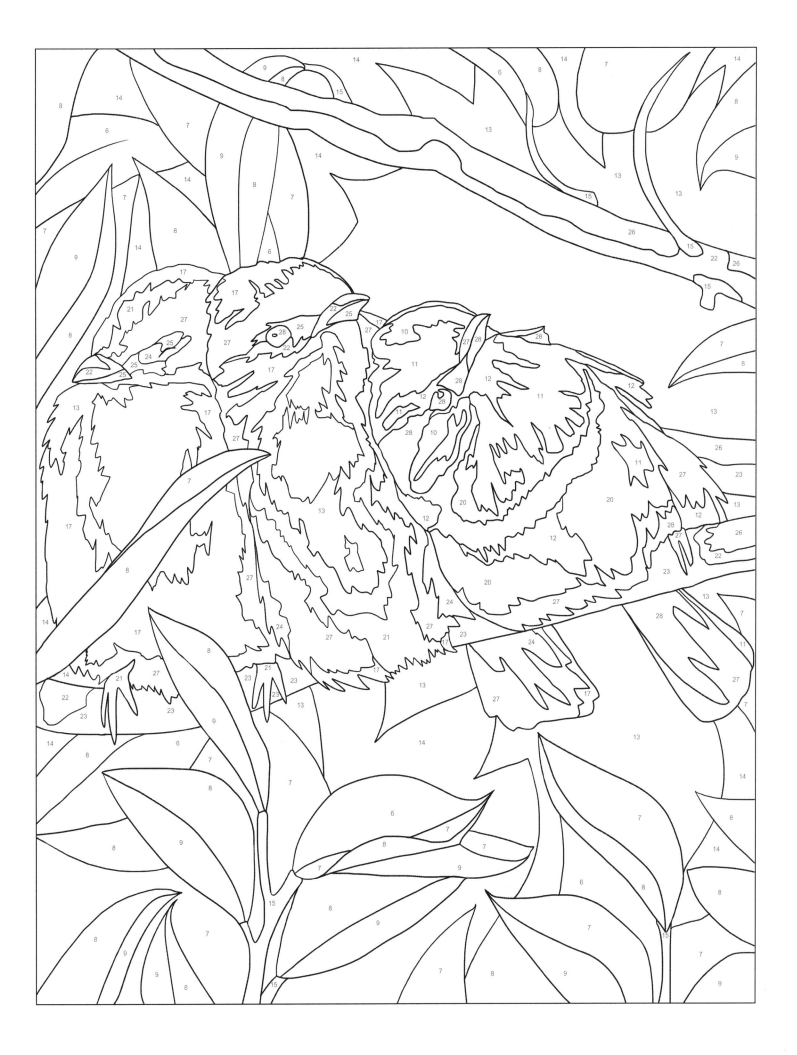

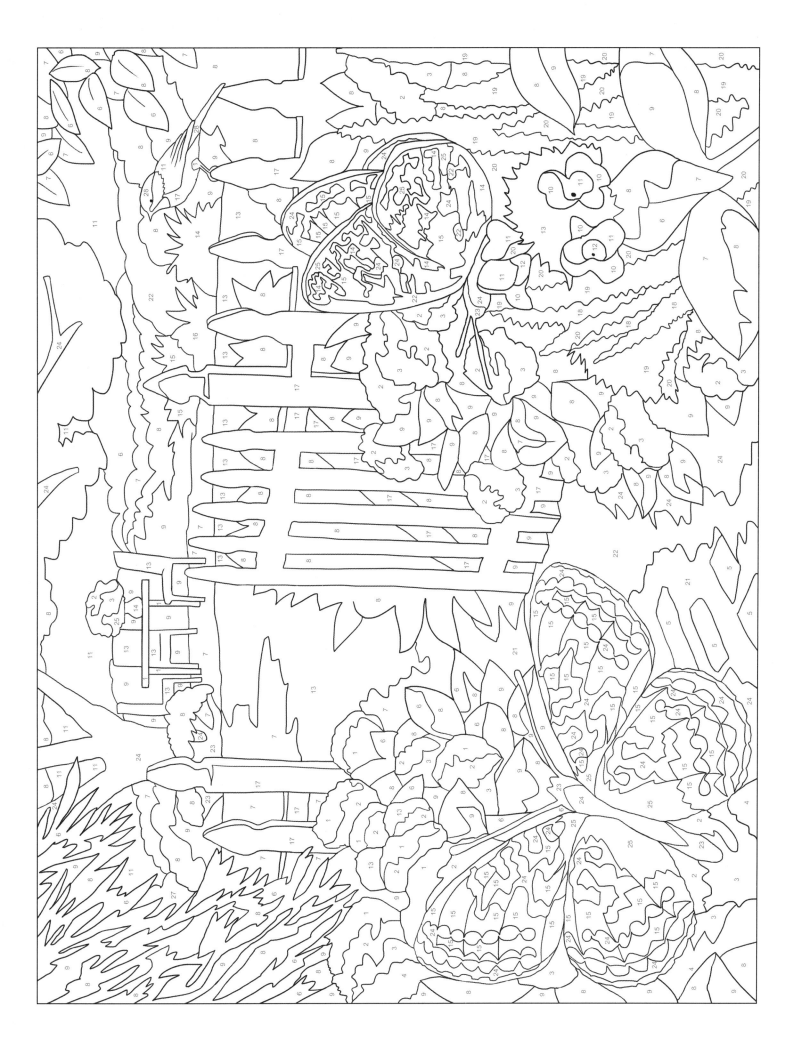

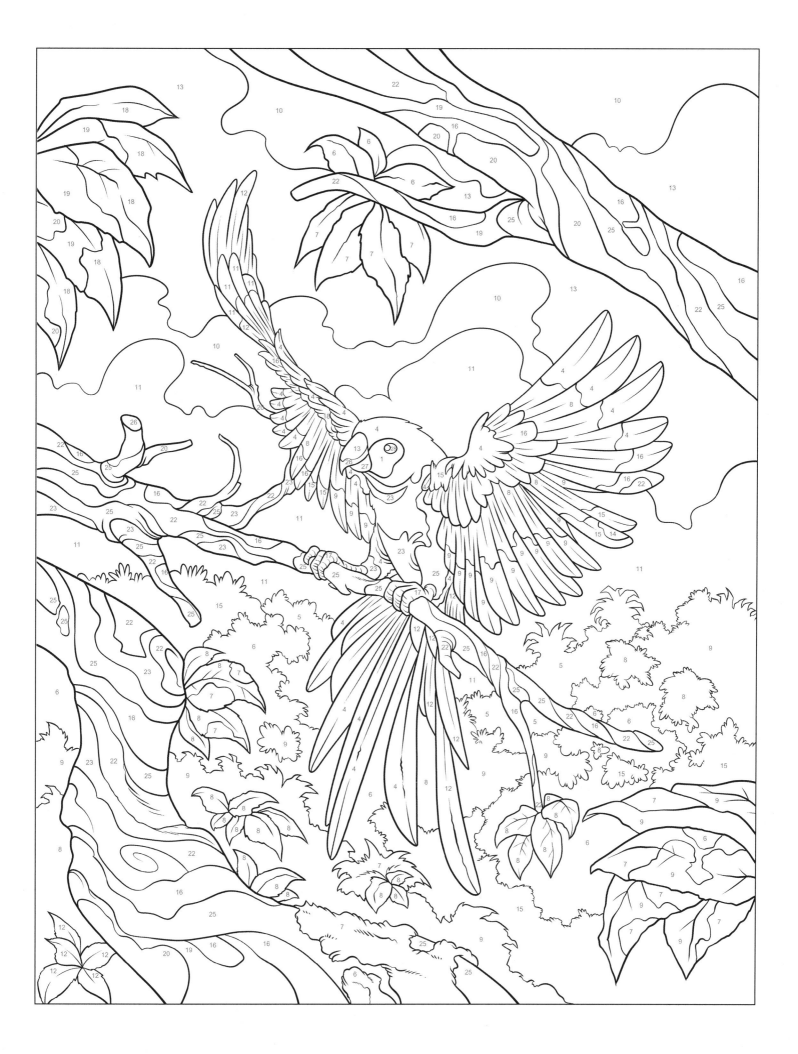

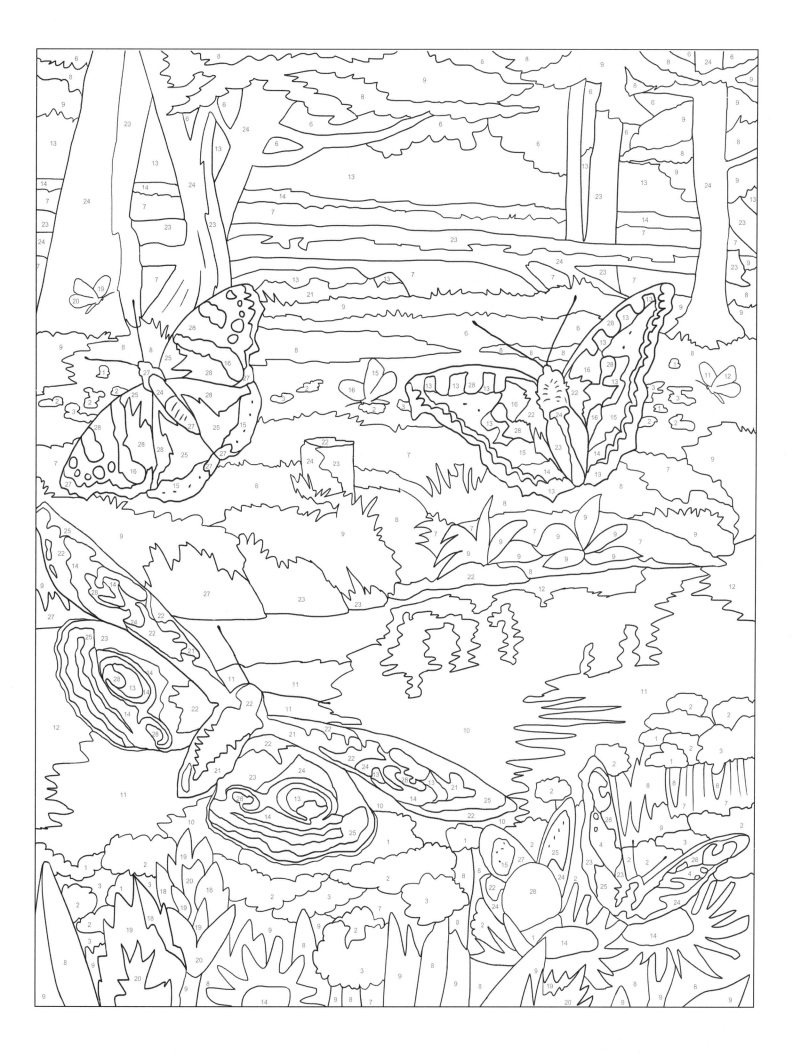

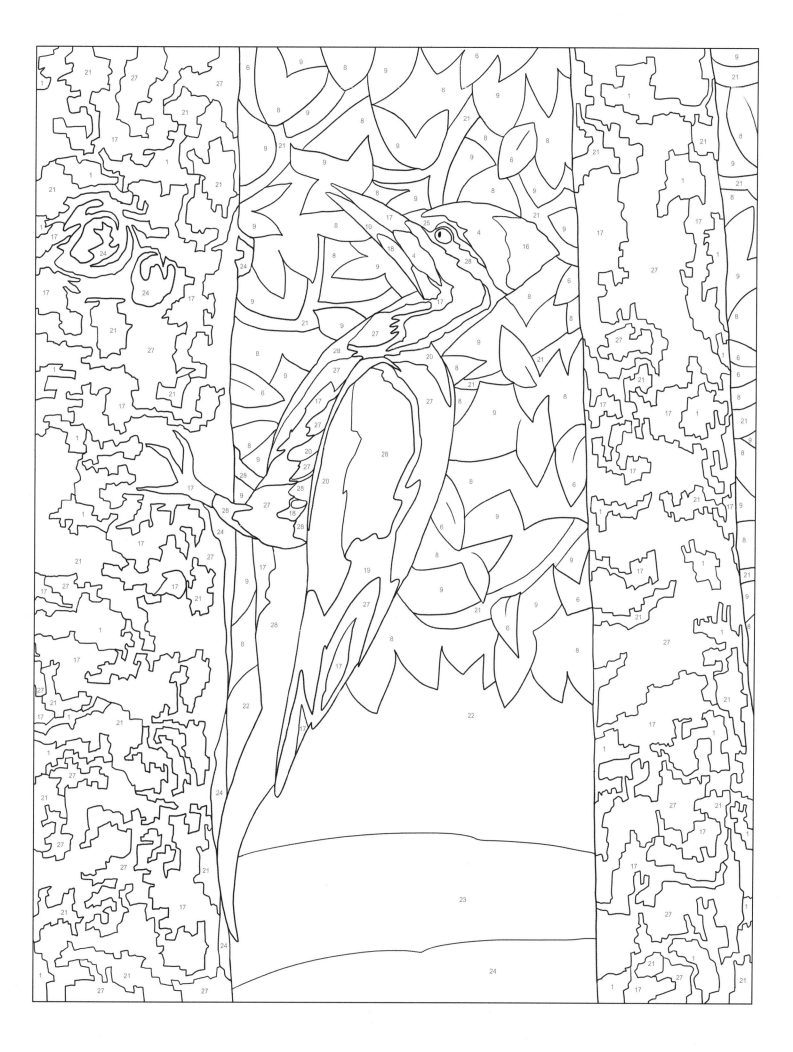

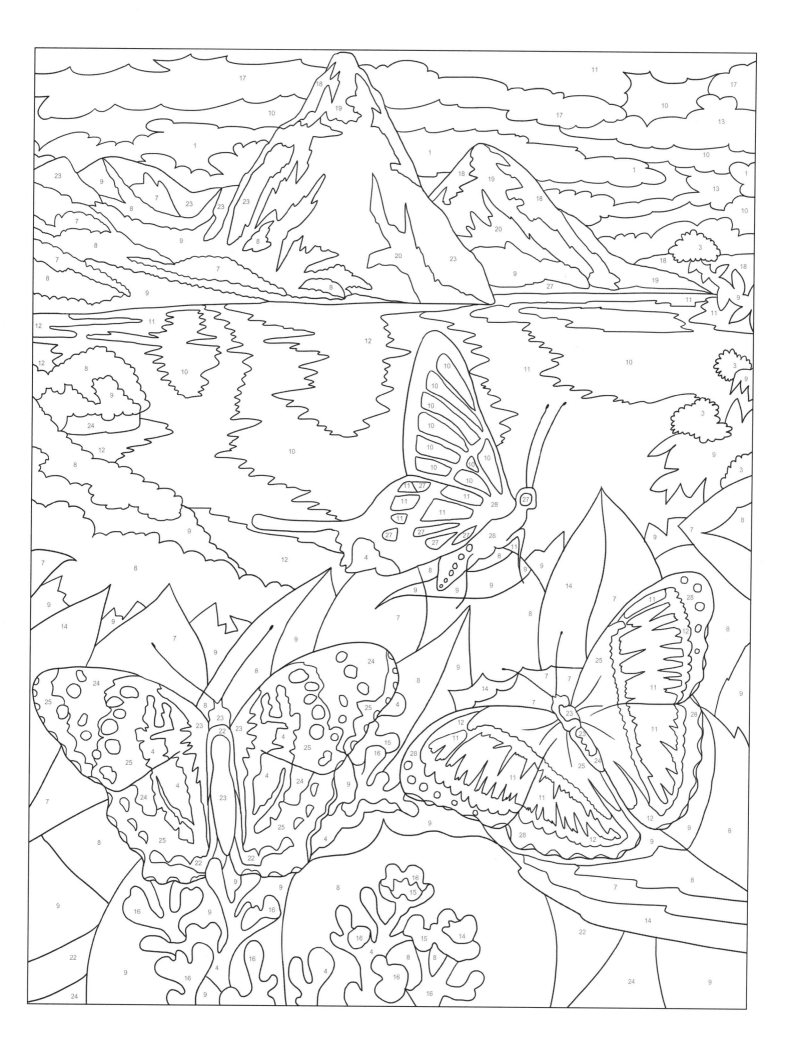

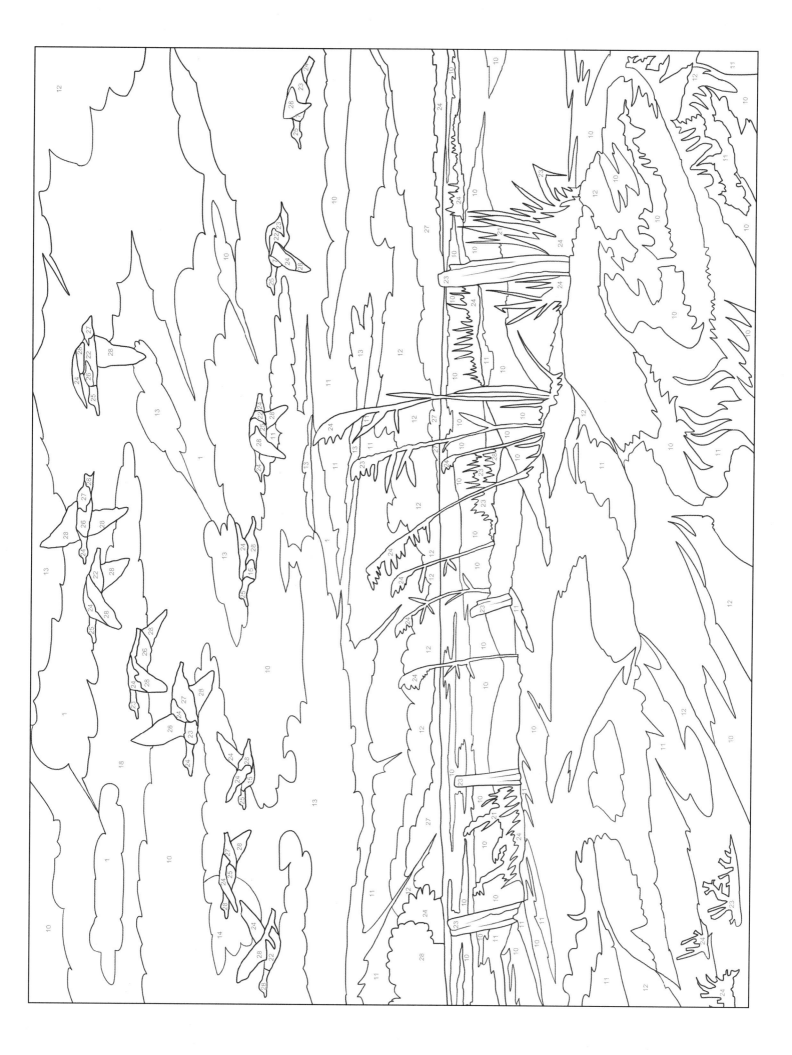

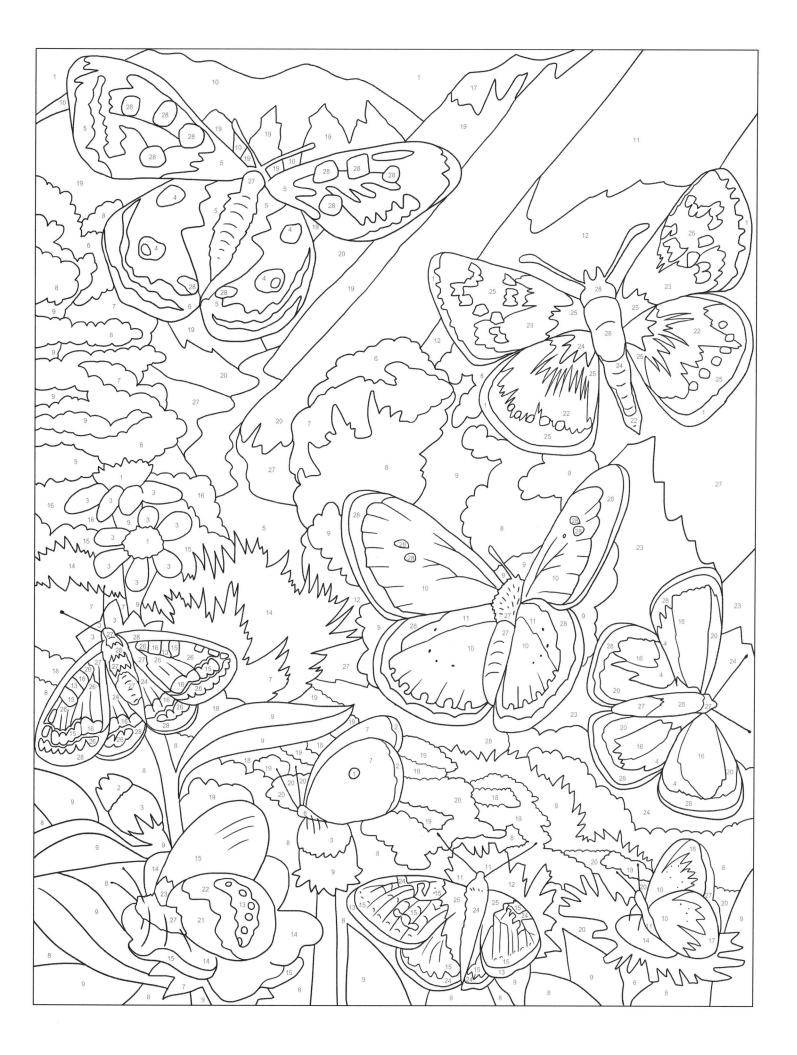

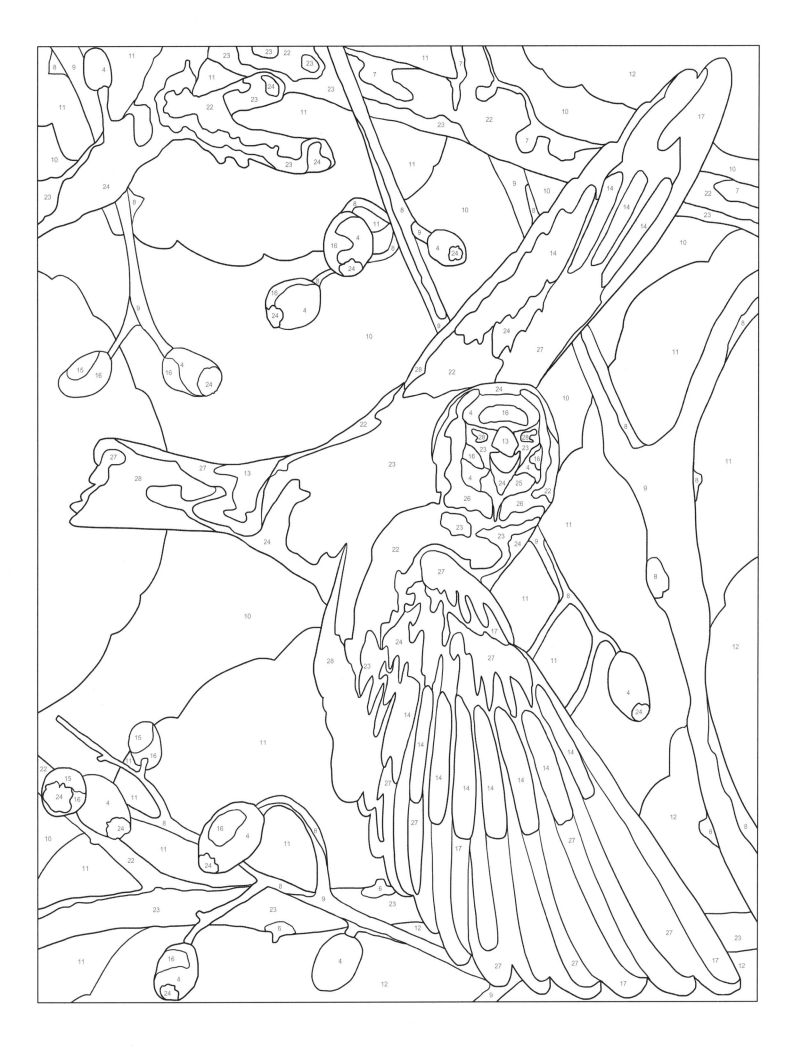

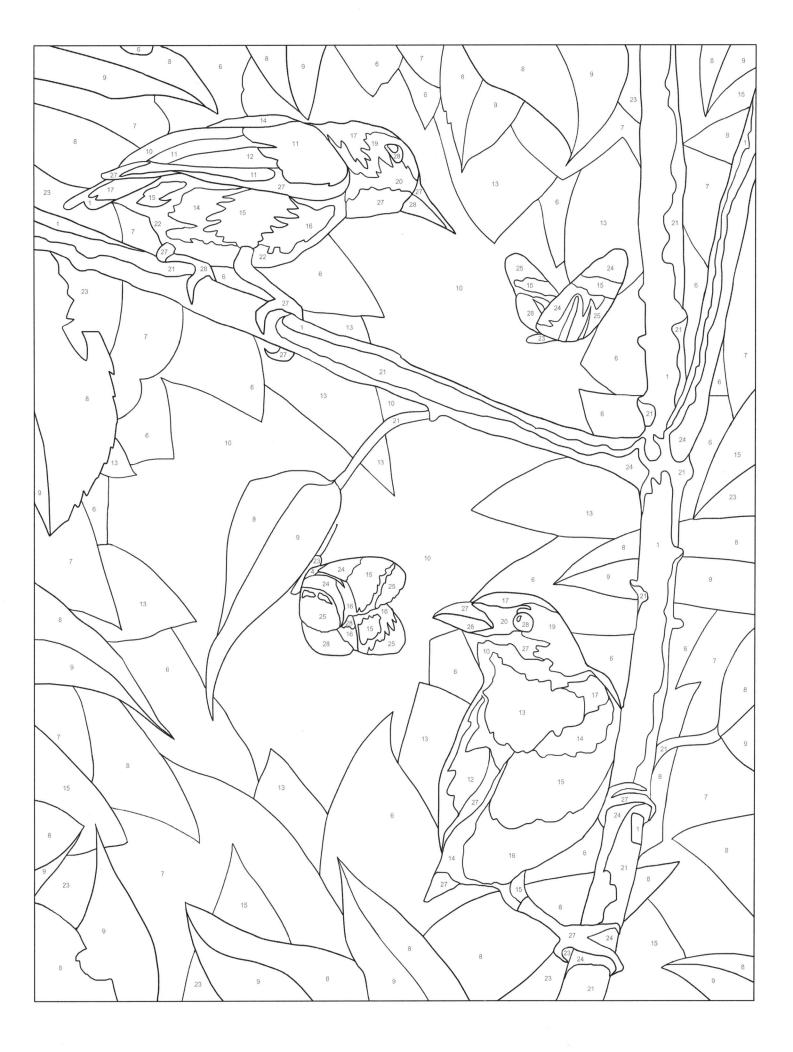

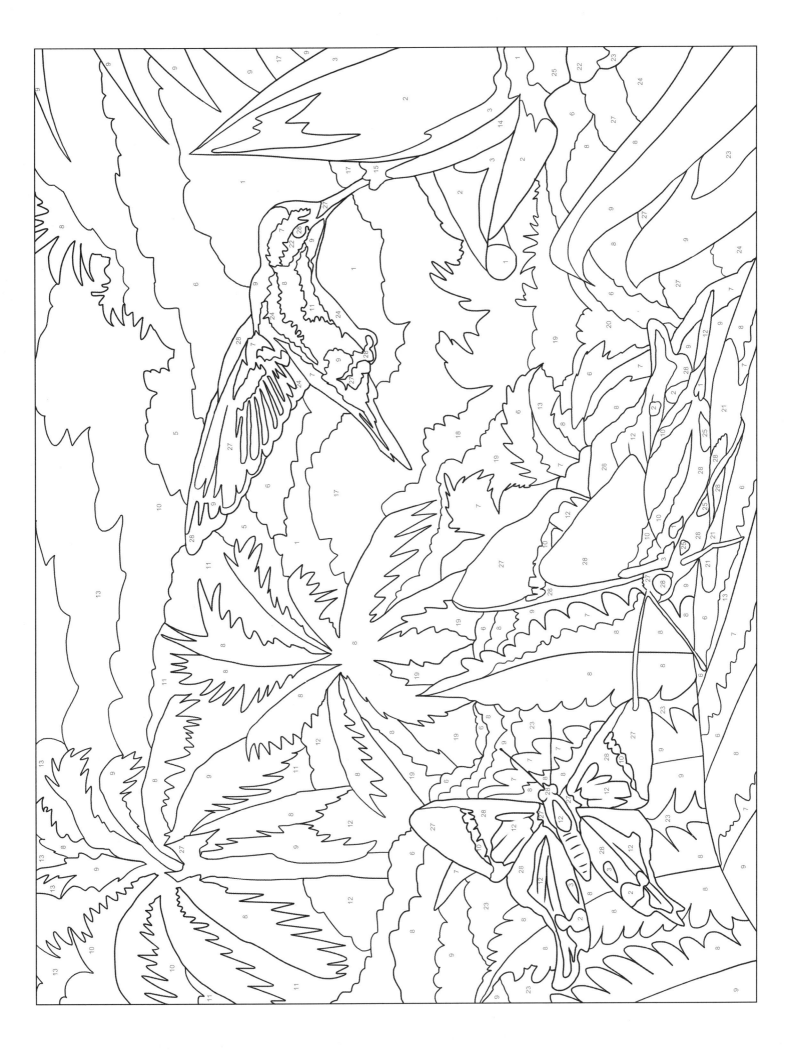

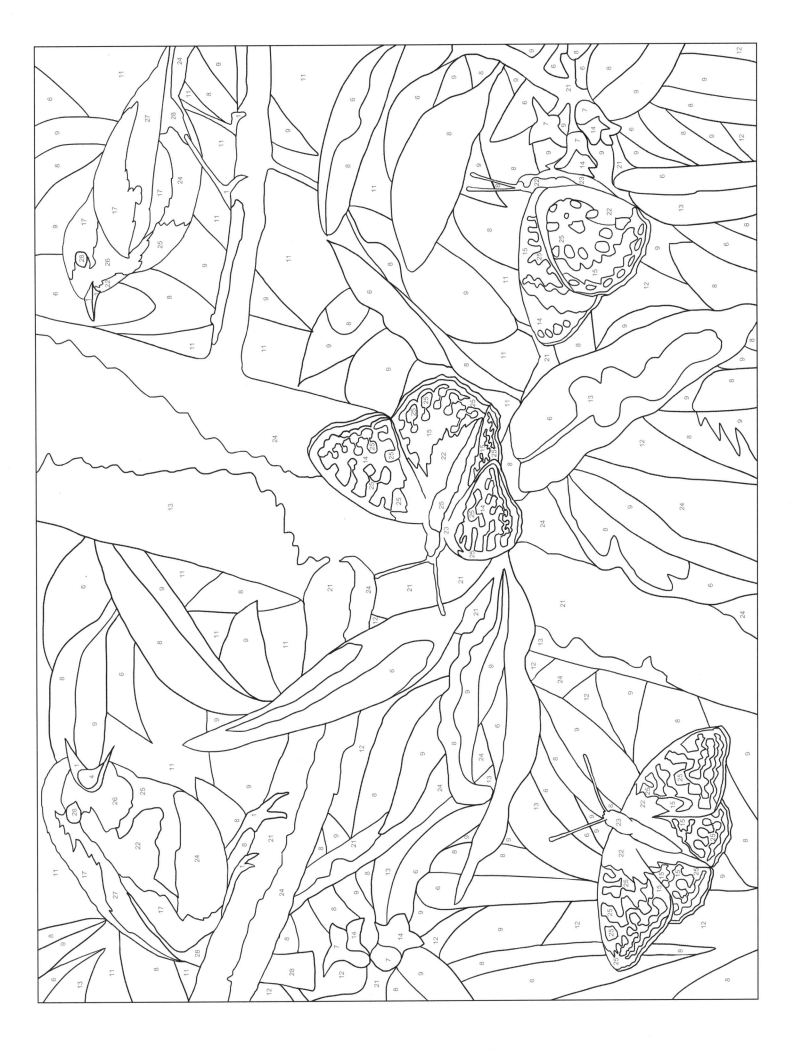

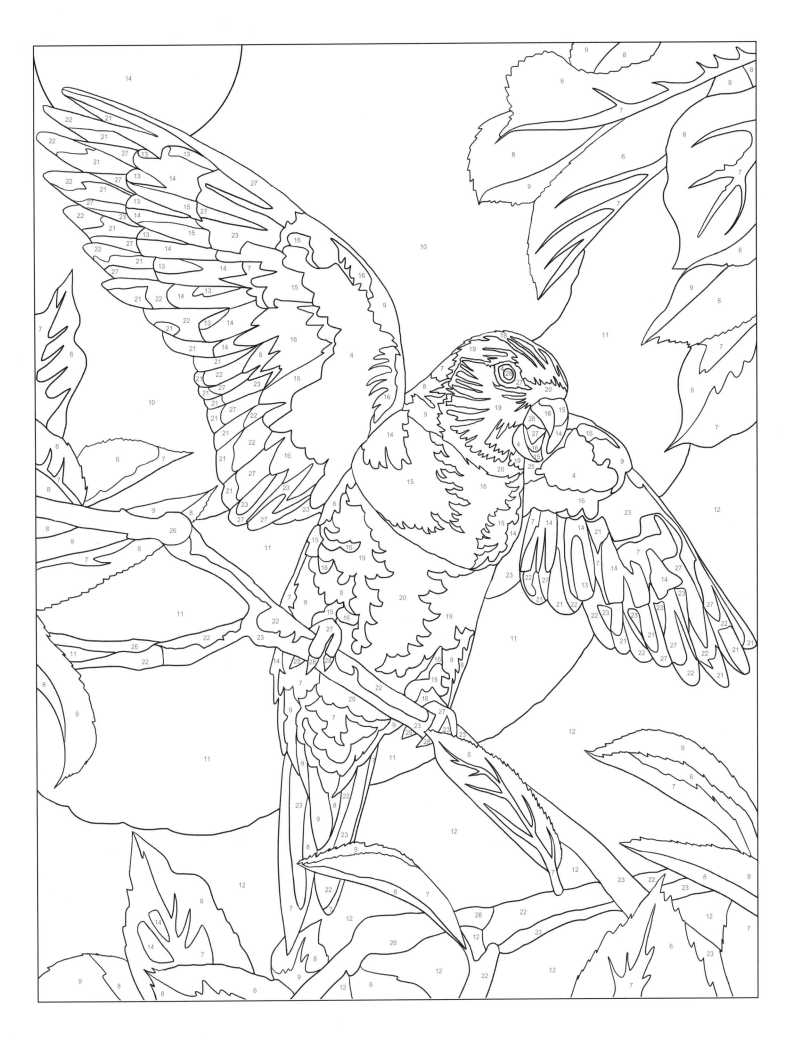

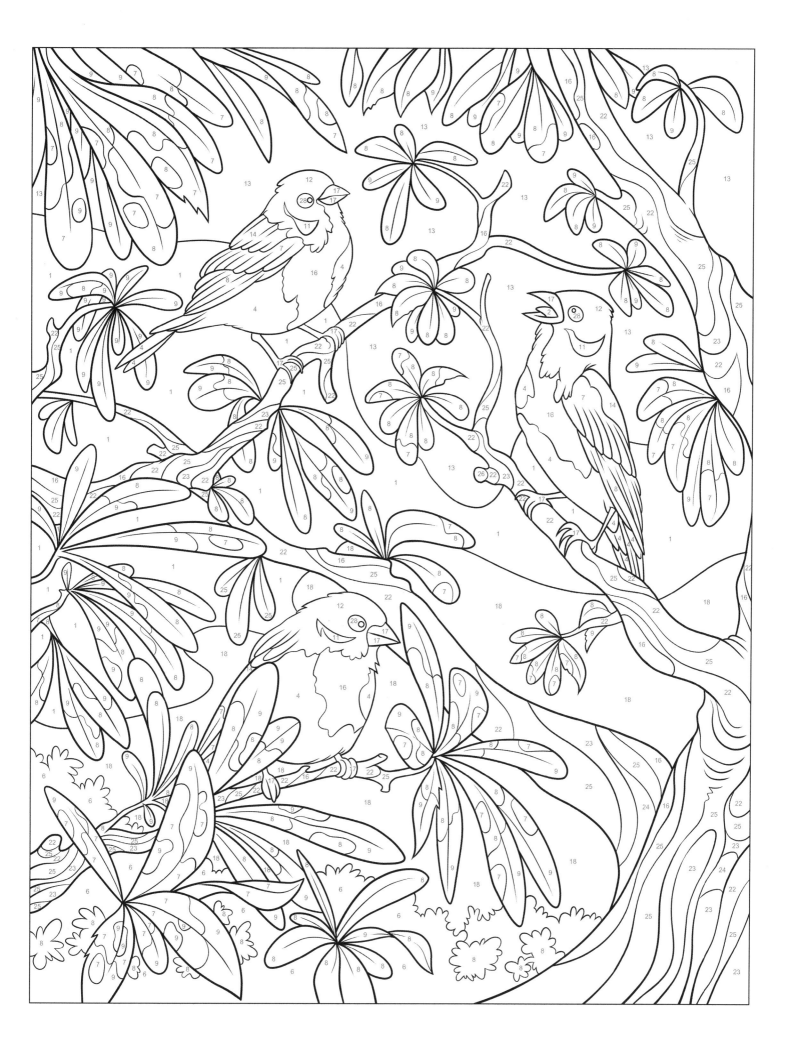

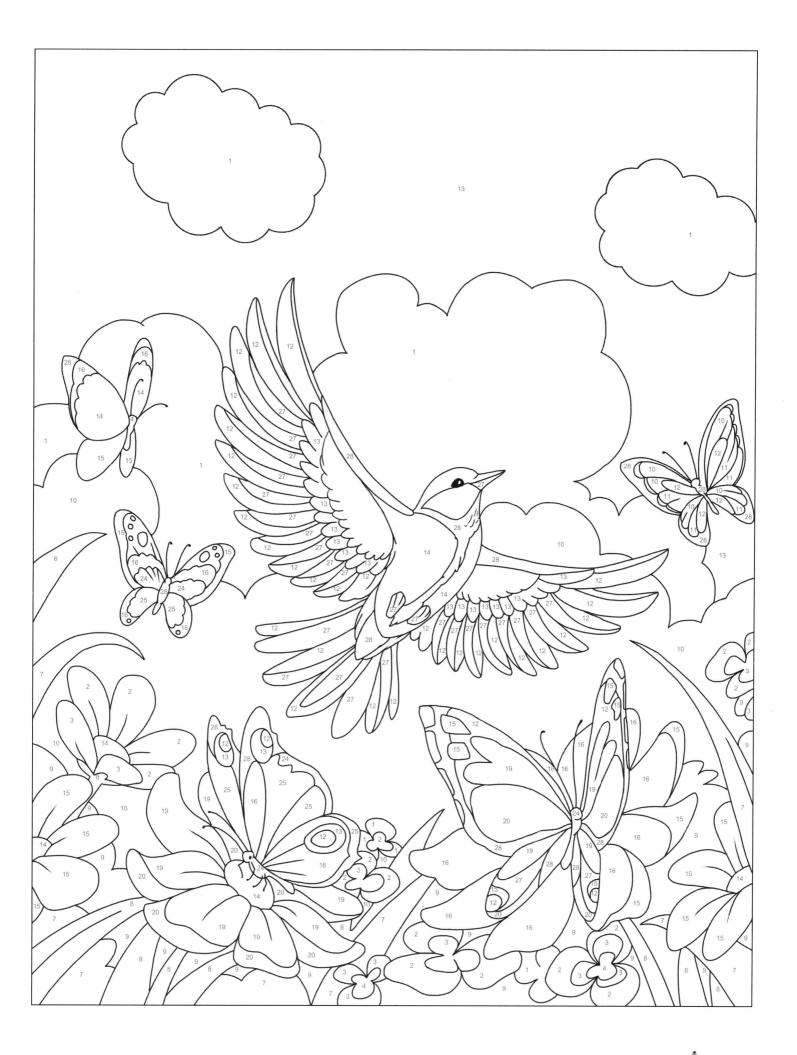

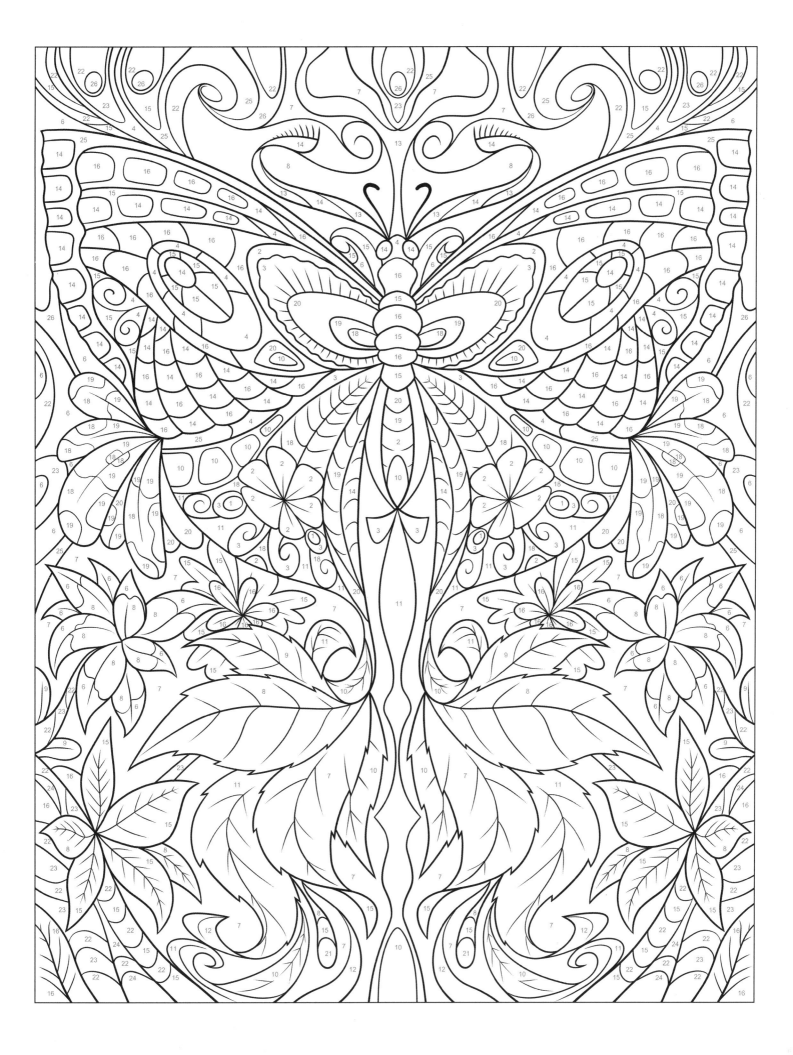

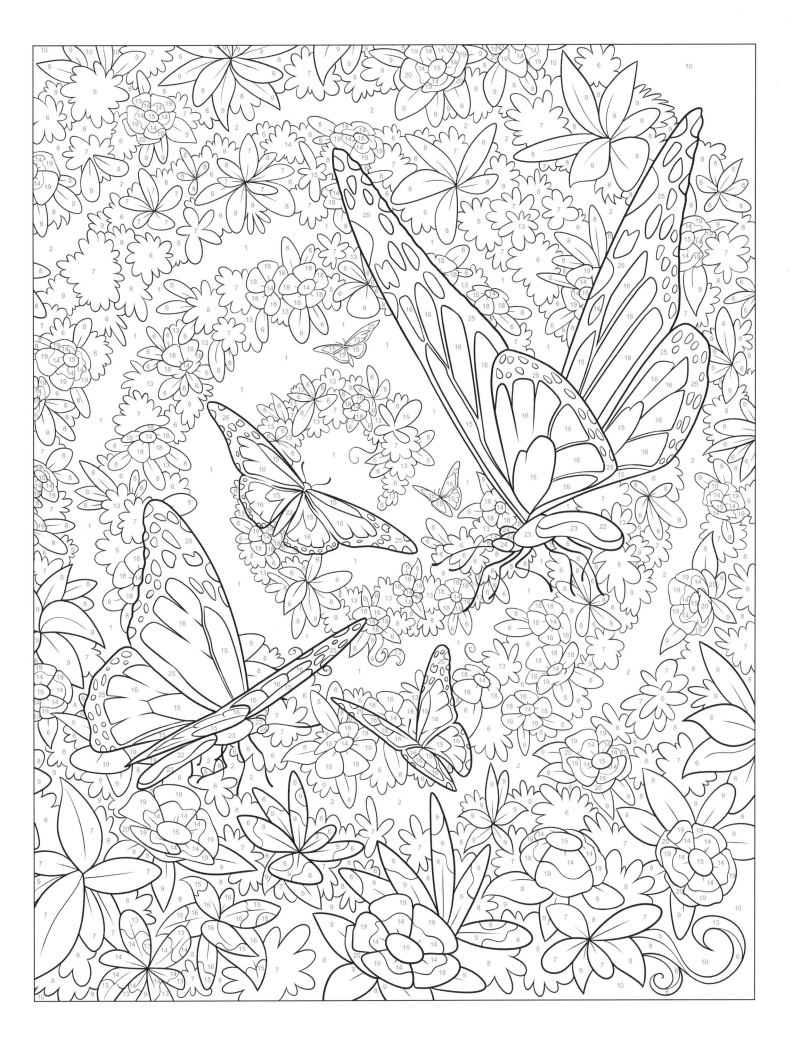

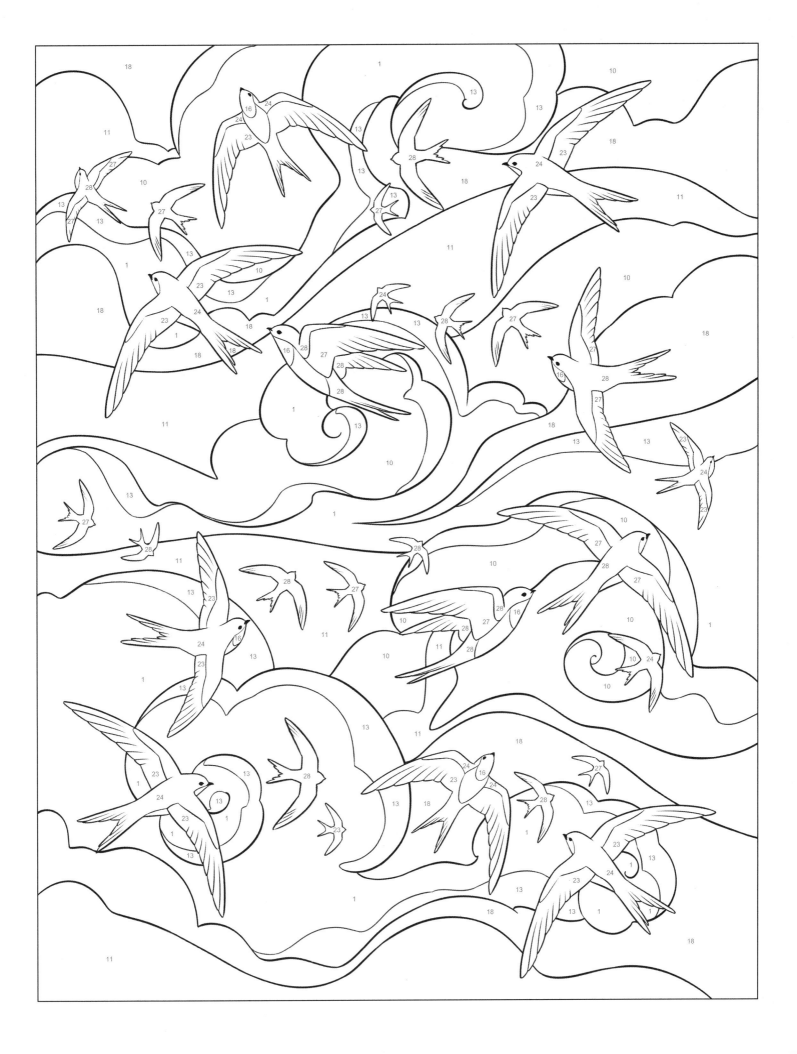

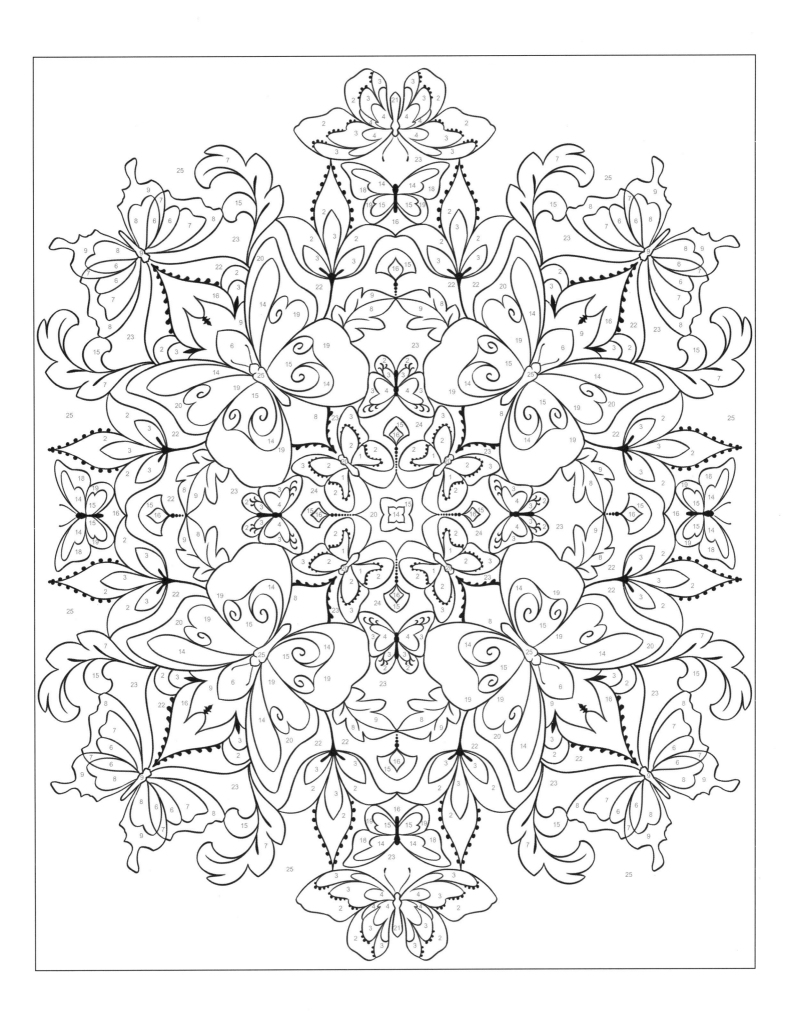

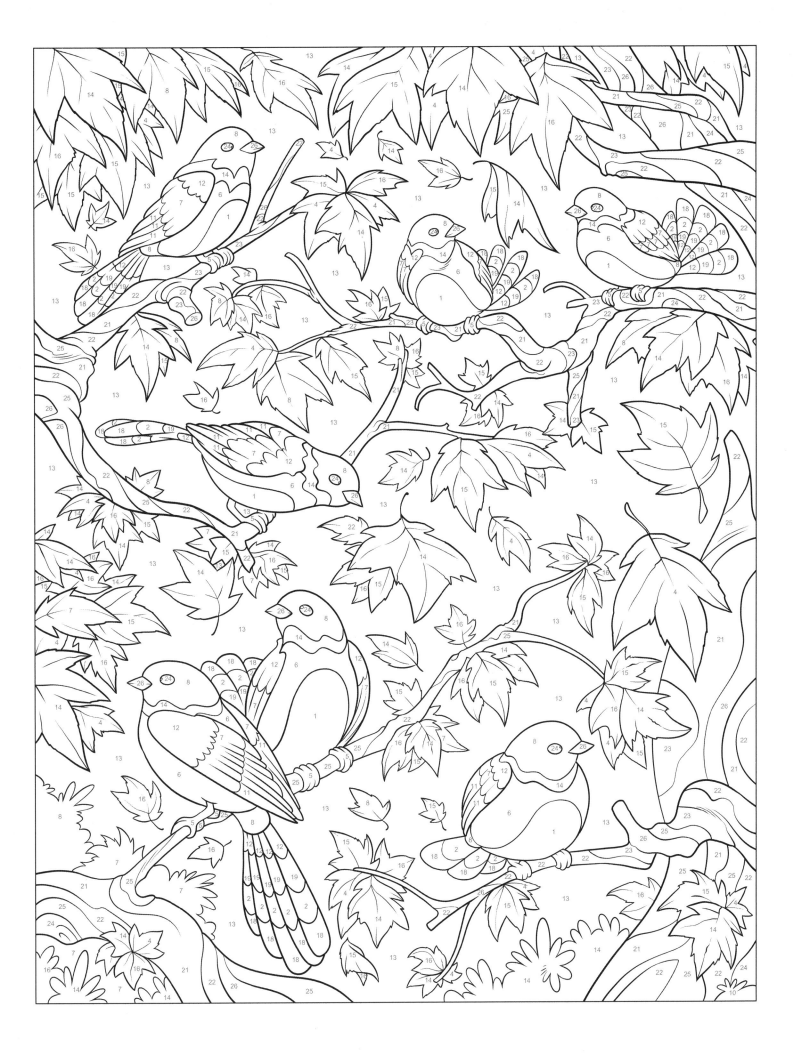

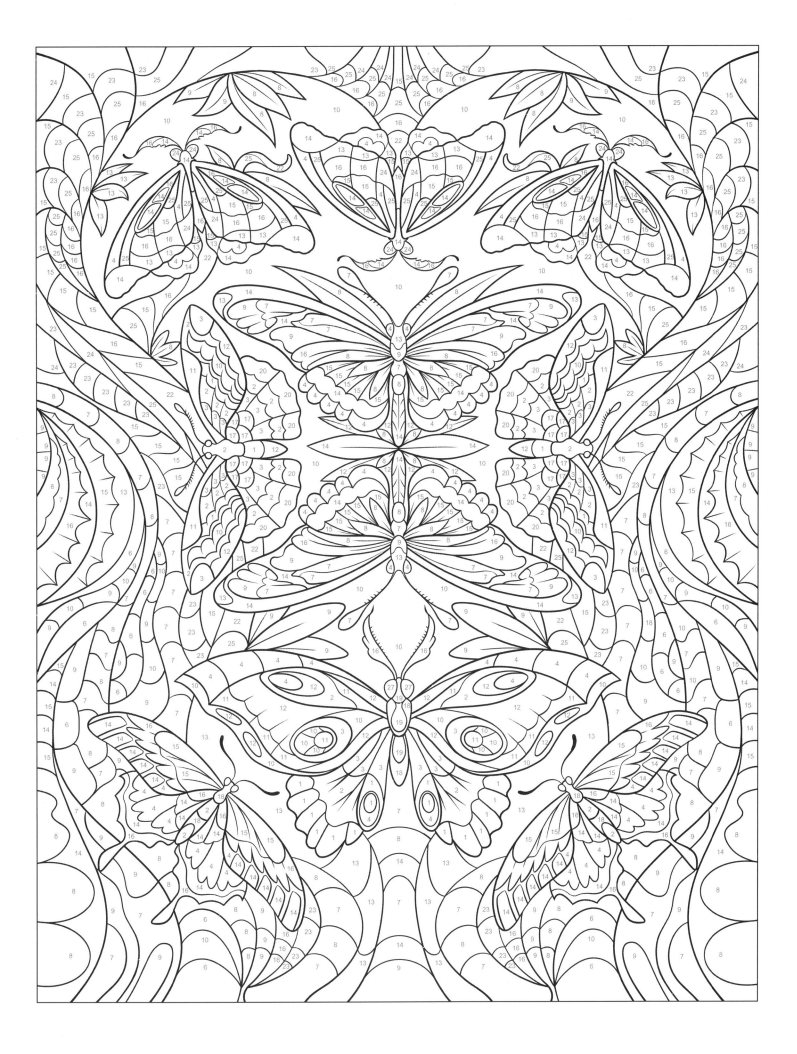

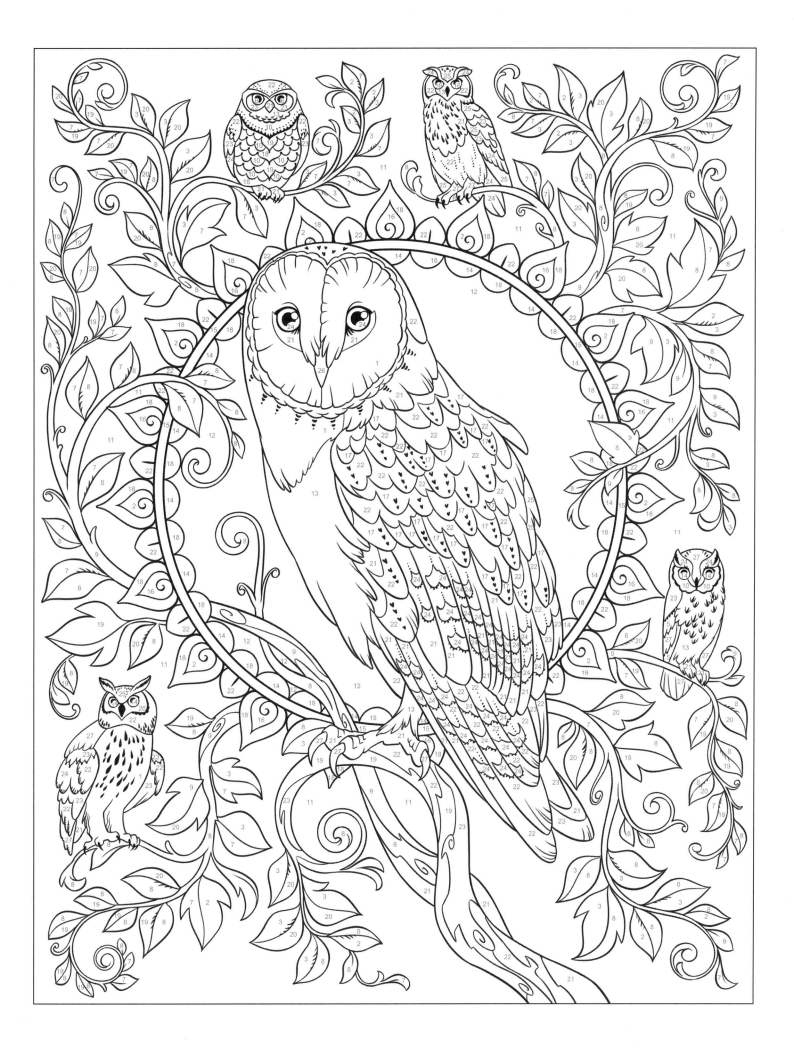

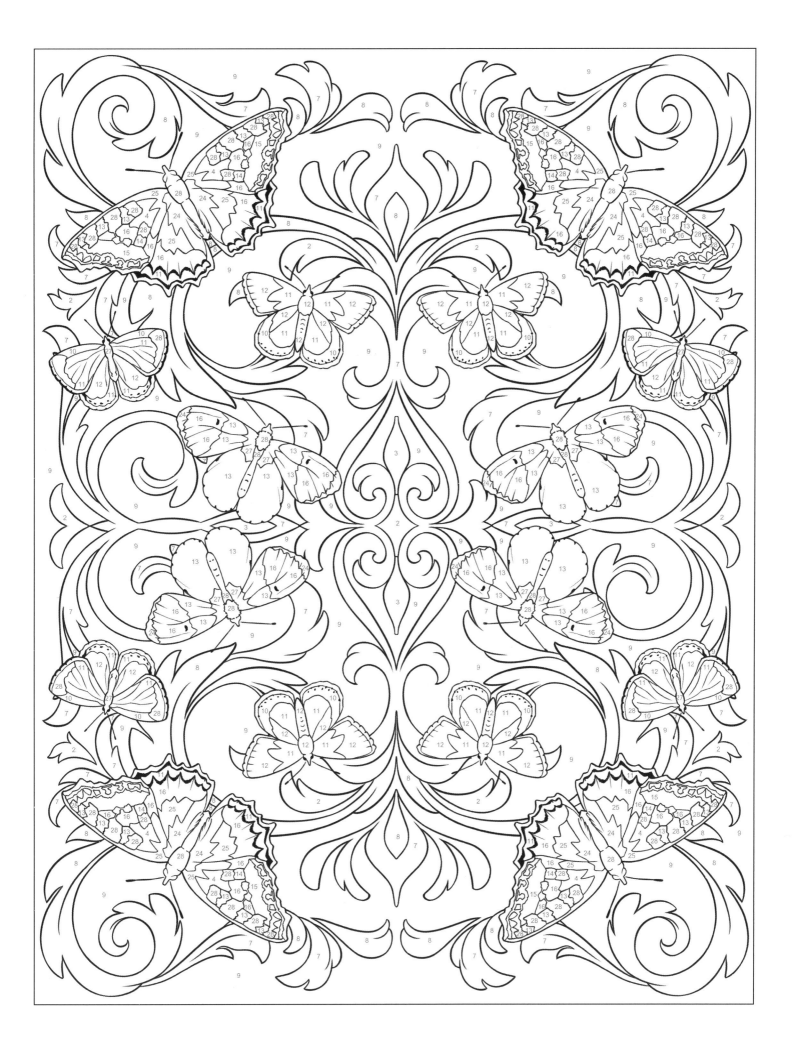

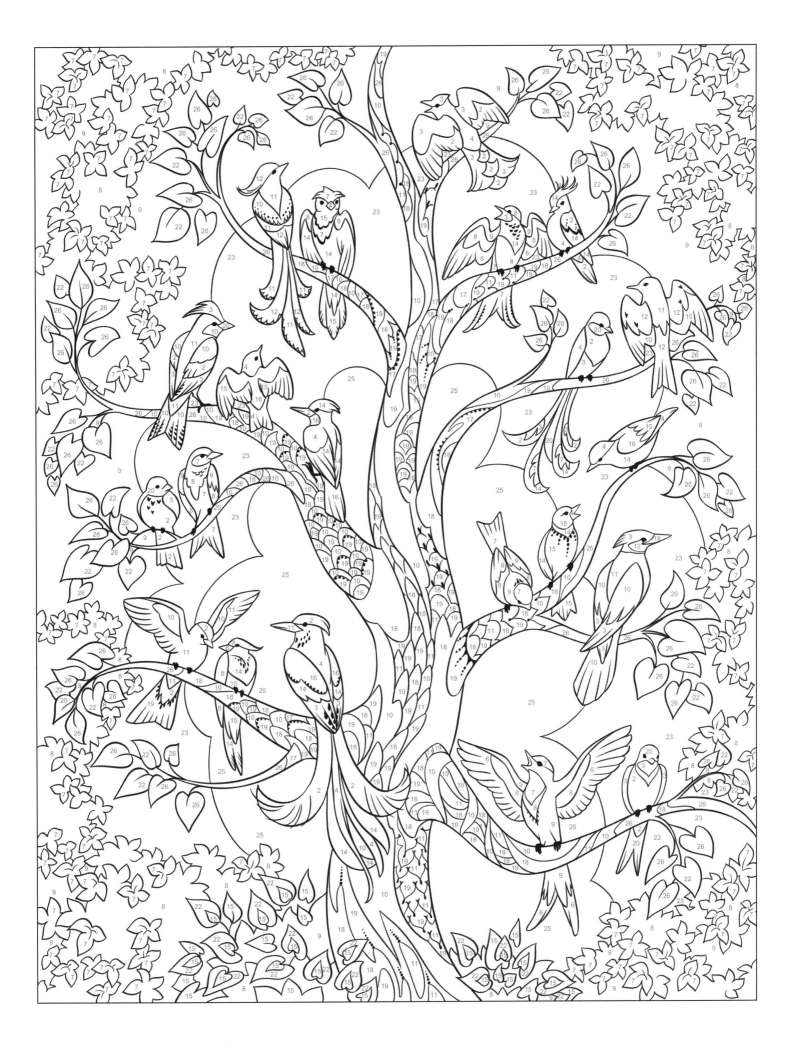

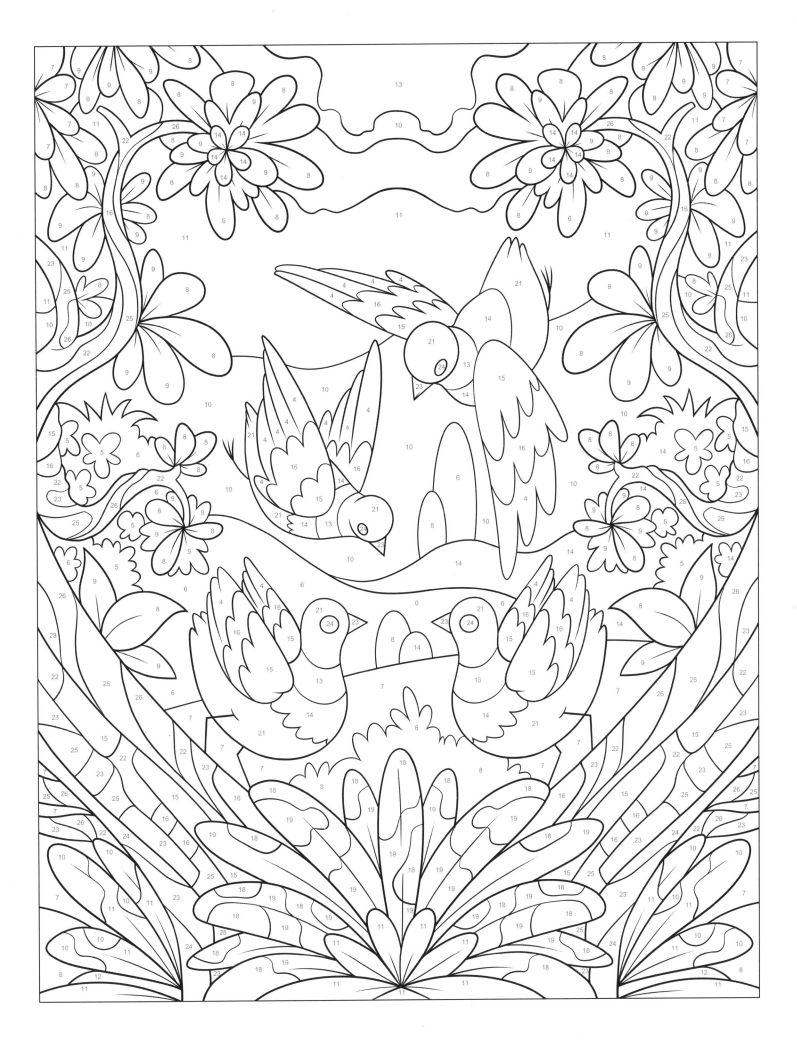

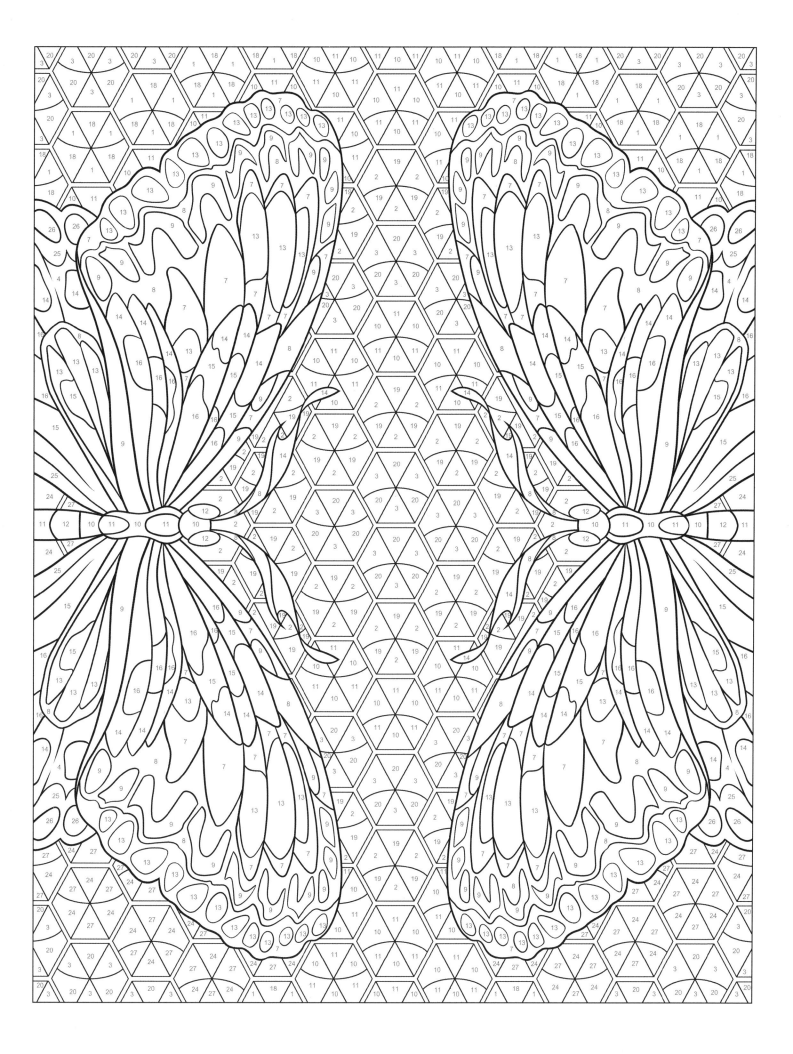

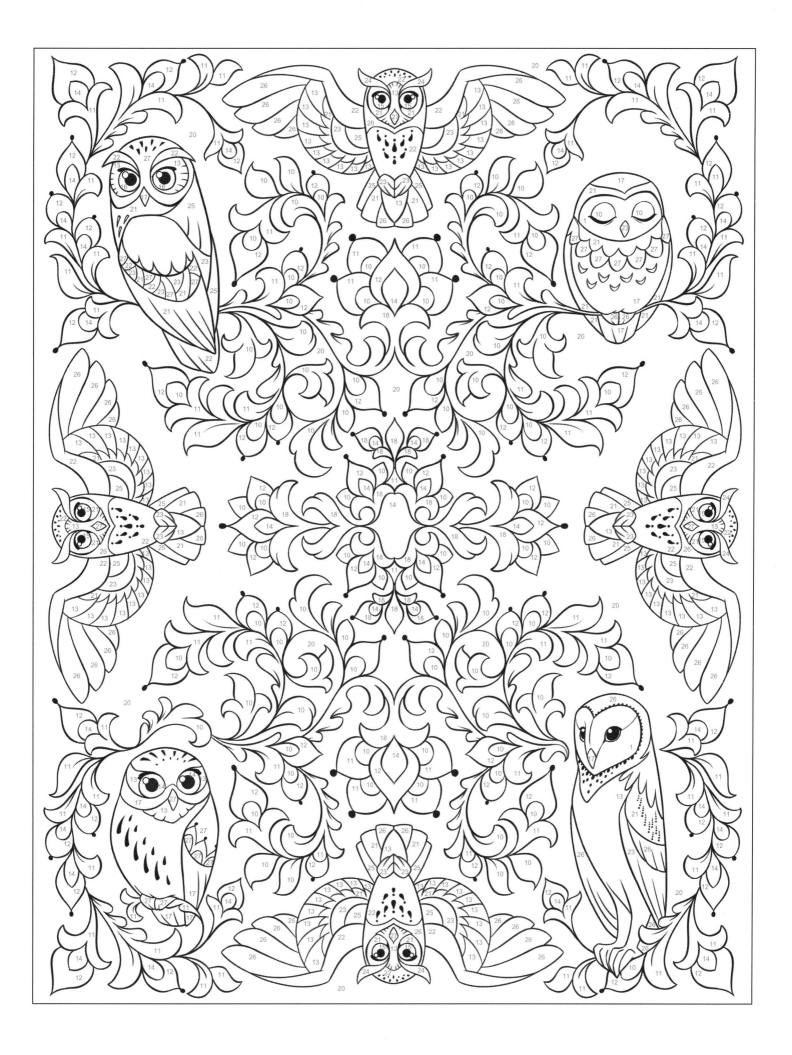

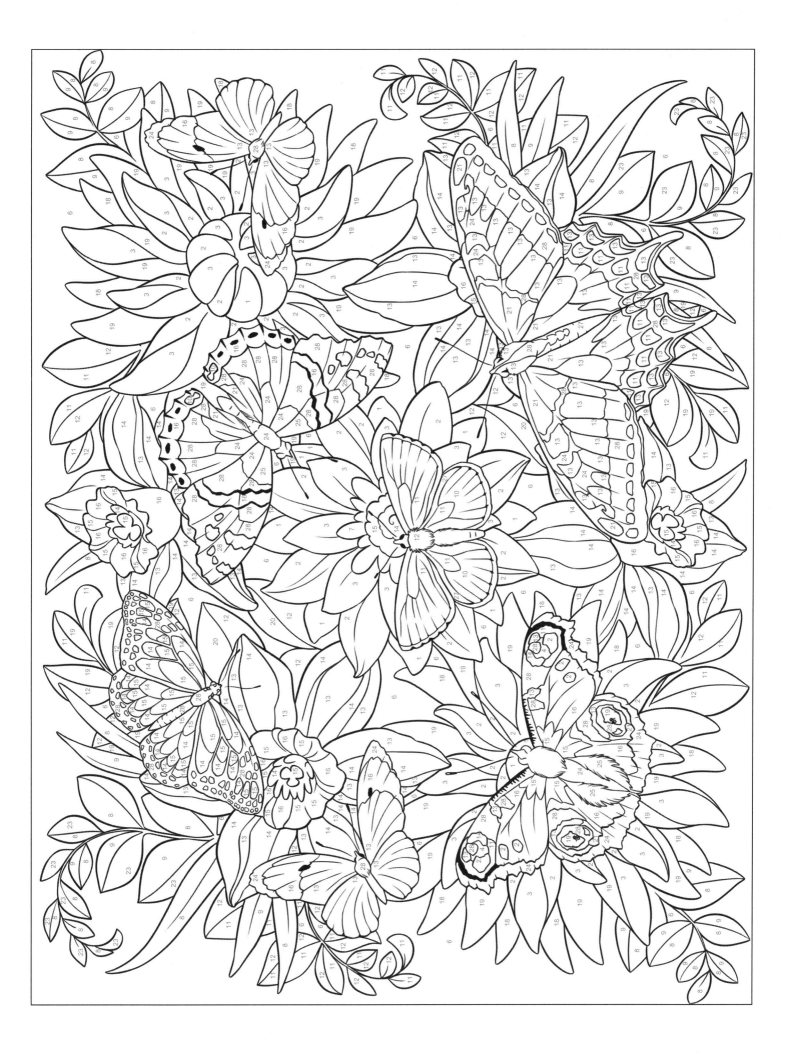

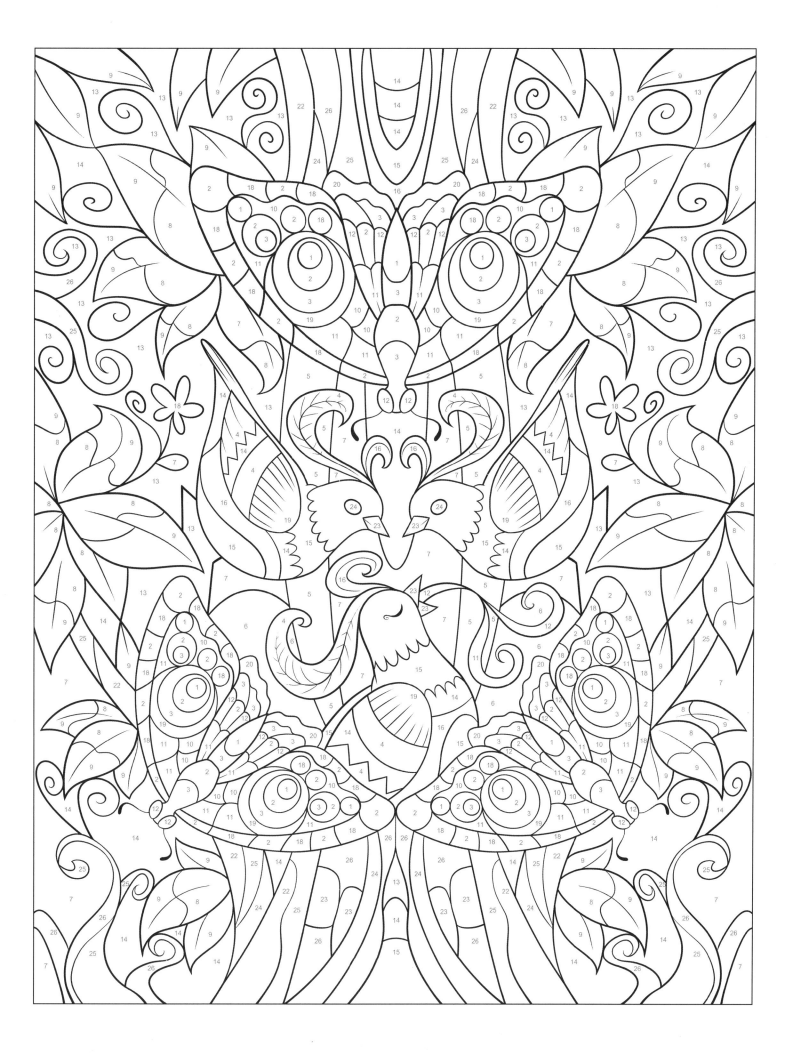